The Day I Fell Off My Bicycle

A Personal Account of Coming to Terms with Quadriplegia

Hilary Crawford

Published in Australia by Sid Harta Publishers Pty Ltd,
ABN: 46 119 415 842
23 Stirling Crescent, Glen Waverley, Victoria 3150 Australia
Telephone: +61 3 9560 9920, Facsimile: +61 3 9545 1742
E-mail: author@sidharta.com.au

First published in Australia 2019
This edition published 2019
Copyright © Hilary Crawford 2019
Cover design, typesetting: WorkingType (www.workingtype.com.au)

The right of Hilary Crawford to be identified as the Author of the Work has been asserted in accordance with the Copyright, Designs and Patents Act 1988.

All rights reserved. No part of this publication may be reproduced, stored in a retrieval system, or transmitted, in any form or by any means without the prior written permission of the publisher, nor be otherwise circulated in any form of binding or cover other than that in which it is published and without a similar condition being imposed on the subsequent purchaser.

Crawford, Hilary
The Day I Fell Off My Bicycle: A Personal Account of Coming to Terms with Quadriplegia
ISBN: 978-1-925230-68-0
pp214

ABOUT THE AUTHOR

Hilary was born in England and at age 18 migrated to Australia in 1963 to be with the rest of her family. She trained as a nurse and was in that profession for 25 years. During this time she graduated both from college and university. She worked in London for a year and then in Switzerland for two years learning to ski and speak French properly. She travelled extensively through Europe, Asia and India. Hilary met David her husband to be in 1974 on a skying trip in Australia. In 1989 she was involved in a serious bicycle accident. At the time she was the team leader of a community rehabilitation service but the accident left her a ventilator dependent quadriplegic. In early 1993 she was diagnosed with breast cancer and died the following year from that disorder.

FOREWORD

Many people have described Hilary as being "brave" and "courageous". Hilary describes herself in this story as someone who just got on with living her life. Two very important aspects of Hilary's character were her ability to live life and her overwhelming love and concern for her fellow humans. Despite all the problems she faced and the extreme level of her disabilities, she worked hard to build the most satisfying and fulfilling life possible.

This was not something new, a character trait developed as a result of her accident, rather it was something which has characterised her whole approach to life. Life may not have been easy, but it was for living. Hilary loved people and was deeply concerned about their welfare. This love was a dominant factor in her working life. One of the things she regretted most after her accident was that she could no longer continue working as a nurse helping other people. Despite that, loving and caring continued to be important aspects of her life. Both of these aspects of Hilary are very evident in this book. I hope you enjoy reading *The Day I Fell Off My Bicycle*.

David Foster | **Strathalbyn, 29 October 1994**

Dedicated to
Freda Mary (Molly) Crawford
(1920 - 2019)
A long life lived so well

One

The Accident

'I continued to drift on feeling incredibly serene, secure and warm.'

It is ironic that I rode my bike all the way from Sydney to Melbourne without any major mishaps, the only issues being a worn chain and a sore knee from pushing too hard one day. Yet three months later I was to have an accident on a quiet Sunday morning which was to dramatically alter mine and my husband's life. How did it happen? My husband, David, and I rode from Marrickville in Sydney where we lived, to Centennial Park. We rode around the park and had breakfast in a café. Then we did another couple of laps, stopped to talk to friends and then rode out of the park. We rode down the road and turned right into the main road.

As we approached Anzac Parade, I slowed down a little as we were intending to turn left at the next set of traffic lights. I was looking ahead deciding whether to speed up as the lights were changing to green when I noticed something black rolling toward me out of the very corner of my eye. Before I had time to register what it was or what direction it was coming from, I came to a sudden and dramatic halt. I looked down and saw a large, thick piece of black truck tyre jammed up between the mudguard and the front wheel of my bike. I found it strangely hard to move as I crashed slowly into the kerb. My hands and feet seemed glued to the bicycle. My head hit the kerb with a resounding crash, but my helmet took the force of the impact.

David stopped a few yards up ahead. 'Are you all right, Hils?' he asked.

'No,' I replied, 'can't breathe.'

Then I started to die. Everything was sepia coloured, like old photographs. There were a whole lot of people elegantly dressed standing around on a lawn drinking champagne out of flute glasses. David was amongst them wearing a cream dinner jacket and bow tie. I walked past him touching him lightly on the arm.

'I love you,' I said.

'I love you too,' he replied.

I noticed one of my colleagues from work. I wonder what he's doing here, I thought. Then I realised that everyone there were people I knew or had known; family, friends and colleagues. I seemed to take it all in at a split-second glance. I recognised a friend who had died some years ago, but this did not seem remarkable. I felt happy to see him. Though I felt tempted to stay, I was in a hurry, and I passed on moving

One   The Accident

swiftly and lightly through a forest of long waving chiffon scarves. I could feel them brushing against my arms, breast and face like a gentle massage. Suddenly I was floating high up in the air. Looking down on the scene of the accident far below, I saw an Intensive Care ambulance stopped near the median strip, its lights flashing and a group of people working on someone lying with their head near the kerb.

I wonder who that is, I thought idly.

I continued to drift on feeling incredibly serene, secure and warm. I had said goodbye to everyone whom I knew and loved. I had said goodbye to myself, Hilary Crawford, and all that that implied. Now it was just me, my spirit (for want of a better word), floating, feeling wonderfully free in the velvety blackness.

'Swallow, swallow!' shouted a raucous voice in my ear.

'Go away,' I thought crossly. 'I don't want to be part of this nightmare. I'm having a beautiful dream.' I returned to the waving scarves.

'Swallow,' the voice persisted. 'Swallow, damn you!'

My throat hurt. *This isn't a nightmare*, I thought with horror, *this is reality.*

The accident came back to me in a rush, and I realised that I was lying on a trolley in casualty. Someone was trying to pass a nasogastric tube (a tube which is passed via the nose into the stomach). With an incredible effort, I let go of the dream and swallowed.

In the meantime, when I had said to David, 'I can't breathe,' he thought, *oh shit. Now I'll have to give mouth to mouth resuscitation, and I've never done it before.* An off-duty nurse and an ambulance driver had seen the accident, and they stopped to help. They immediately started mouth to mouth resuscitation. A few minutes later an Intensive Care ambulance on the way to another accident stopped to render assistance. I was taken to the nearest hospital where I woke up.

I tried to open my eyes but everything was so bright, and I closed them again. People were talking, I think it was about me, but I did not really take in what they were saying. I swallowed again, and my throat hurt. Then I realised that I had an endotracheal tube in place and someone was hand-ventilating me. (An endotracheal tube is a short tube which is passed via the nose or the mouth down into the air passage or trachea. In my case, it had been connected to an airbag and someone was pumping air into my lungs by hand. Then I remembered that I could not breathe. I was lifted on a frame onto a trolley and wheeled out to an ambulance. I could feel the sun on my face and tried to open my eyes again, but the light hurt. A male voice advised me to keep my eyes closed as the sun was very bright. I was now in the ambulance being driven very slowly and carefully.

I must have injured my spine, I thought and tried to move my arms and legs, but nothing happened. Then I tried to judge what I could feel, but I could only feel the slat of the frame under my head. I was puzzled. Surely, I should feel more than that? I experienced no pain, just a nothingness where my body was. It was very strange, so I decided to wait until we reached our destination to sort this out. People were talking to me, mostly a young female voice telling me that everything was all right, explaining that I had an accident and that I was being taken to one of the spinal injuries units. I realised that she was one of the paramedics and that she was the person who was hand-ventilating me.

I felt quite calm and secure. There were two male voices, one of them David's. I felt reassured and glad that he was with me. It reminded me of the time when I was taken to hospital at the age of four with scarlet fever and I realised that my father was in the ambulance with me. It was the same comforting feeling. I thought about that time and about other pleasant memories and then about the accident. From time to time I opened my eyes and then closed them and drifted off to sleep. Once when I opened my eyes, David was peering into my face.

'Are you all right?' he asked anxiously

I tried to smile at him and mumbled something incoherent in reply.

Soon we arrived at our destination; it was a room with cream coloured walls. The paramedics were talking to two young doctors about me. The doctors also asked David about some of my personal details and about the accident. Then there was a discussion as to how best to ventilate me while tests were carried out. I noticed that I had an intravenous infusion in my arm. Then I was inside the smooth grey tunnel of a CAT scan machine. I had often wondered what it was like to be scanned.

I awoke again in a ward; there was a babble of voices, a soft Irish brogue amongst them. Then I was being lifted again onto a bed and the frame was removed. I was pleased because the slat was hurting the back of my head. I was told that I was being connected to a respirator which would feel different to the hand-ventilation. It was, but after a couple of minutes I felt quite comfortable. There were a lot of lights and noise from machinery, and I wondered whether I was in the spinal unit. Almost as if they had read my thoughts, someone told me that I was in Intensive Care and gave the name of the hospital. After a while, the curtains were drawn back and David was there looking anxious. I tried to smile at him reassuringly before drifting off to sleep again

Two

Intensive Care

As long as you need me.

When I awoke the following day, I remembered that I was in hospital and recalled the details of my accident. I looked down at my body lying there so lifeless and still. So very different from the active person I was yesterday.

I'm a nurse with many years' experience including intensive care work. However, for eleven years prior to the accident, I worked as a community nurse. At the time of my accident, I was team leader of a community rehabilitation service which provides a service to people with physical disabilities who live in an inner west area of Sydney. It was an interesting and busy job. As team leader, I was responsible for the day to day administration of a multidisciplinary team of health professionals and support staff. I was involved with community development and sat on various committees. I also carried a clinical load and saw clients at home for assessment, follow up counselling, education and support. With other staff members, I ran two groups, a Stress Management Group and a Stroke Group for clients who had suffered a stroke, along with their friends or relatives. As well as this I saw clients in the clinic and accompanied the medical director on rounds in the hospital.

I'm married to David Foster (I kept my own name when we married). He's an accountant and a year before he had started a new job as a manager of the finance sector with an insurance company. It was a well-paid job with good job prospects. We have no children as I am infertile. We lived in a small semi-detached house in Marrickville which we were buying and recently had paid off a second mortgage. David and I enjoyed doing many things together such as cycling, skiing, bushwalking and camping. We travelled extensively and had plans to do more. We were both studying. David was in the middle of a Master of Business Administration Course, and I had just re-enrolled to complete the final year of a Graduate Diploma of Administration.

All that changed because of my accident. It was like going to step on board a ferry which was taking me to a known destination only to end up in the water. Here I was lying flat on my back in a hospital bed. The next three days were rather hazy as I drifted in and out of sleep. Nurses introduced themselves and attended to my care, washing me, suctioning (removing) secretions from my trachea, attending to the intravenous infusion, among other things. I noted that I had a urinary catheter

Two   Intensive Care

(a tube which is passed via the urethra into the bladder). I wondered when it had been put in as I had no recollection.

Every few hours I was lifted on the frame to relieve the pressure on my back. This was uncomfortable, and I was always relieved to be placed back on the bed. Doctors examined me and asked what I could feel and what I could move. It did not seem silly to be asked to move limbs which did not respond as I was very familiar with this sort of neurological examination through attending clinics at work. I met Professor Nguyen, a gentle, softly spoken man who was in charge of the Intensive Care unit. He explained that I had an accident and had damaged my spinal cord. He also talked about the endotracheal tube in my throat and the respirator that was helping me to breathe.

Paul, the medical director of the rehabilitation service where I worked, came to see me. He looked shocked and worried.

'I've contacted Helen,' he said. I looked at him alarmed. 'I felt that it was best under the circumstances,' he added.

'Oh no,' I thought, 'poor Helen. I've stuffed things up for her again.'

Helen, an occupational therapist, was second in charge of the team. Three times she had enrolled to do a management course at the education centre at this hospital. Last time she cancelled the course because of me and now this. I felt really bad.

Peter went on, 'I've spoken to Professor Chalker, he's in

charge of the Spinal Injuries Unit. He's a colleague of mine and has a very high reputation. I've told him all about you.'

I mumbled thanks. Work was uppermost on my mind as I had a very busy schedule mapped out for the next month. We would have to cancel the groups which I was about to start. I thought perhaps Helen could send my apologies to the meetings but what about the team's annual general meeting scheduled for next month? I became concerned.

Helen arrived in the afternoon looking anxious. She was used to talking to people with speech difficulties and asked me mainly yes or no questions, which was a relief as it was hard to talk with the endotracheal tube in my throat. I told her that all my appointments were in my diary which was on the desk at work. Helen told me not to worry, but I did anyway. She returned the following day to give me a report on what was happening.

David was there much of the time sitting by the bed, stroking my head or holding my hand. He looked tired and drawn.

'Don't worry Hils, I'll look after you,' he said

I thought, *let's hope that won't be necessary.* I tried to smile and wished there was something that I could say to him.

On the third day, I was awake and alert and ready to take stock of my situation. I was unable to move my legs or arms, and I could feel nothing below the neck. Obviously, I had broken my neck and damaged my spinal cord, but I did not know whether I would make any improvement. I hoped I would recover use of my hands. I was on a respirator to help me breathe, and I wondered how long I would need it because I disliked the thought of being kept alive on a machine. I toyed with the idea of turning it off and had I been able to I would have reached out and done so. Then I thought about asking the medical or nursing staff if they would help me but realised they could not do so for all sorts of reasons. Then I hoped it would not be too long before I recovered my breathing.

My throat hurt, saliva collected in my mouth but it took an effort to swallow it, and my tongue felt dry and furred despite the frequent times the nurses cleaned my mouth. I was very aware of the endotracheal tube, and I thought of the people that I had nursed with such tubes in place. I had never realised how uncomfortable they were. In addition to this, I had a nasogastric tube draining the gastric juices from my stomach. I had an intravenous infusion in both arms and a catheter into my bladder draining my urine into a bag hanging on the side of the bed. I could see the shocked expression on my visitors' faces and could imagine how I appeared to them. Me lying flat on my back with a thick tube in my mouth which was connected by more tubing to a machine; another tube in my nose draining green fluid into a bag and two hanging bottles of fluid supplying the tubes in my arms. Very different from the active, able-bodied person when they last saw me.

I had strange body sensations which were to persist for several months. My hands were a mass of twisted, knotted and jangled nerves. Though I knew my arms were lying flaccidly beside my body, they felt as though they were lying across my body. When I slept they felt as if they were wrapped tightly around me, almost as though I was protecting myself. Often, I felt as though my whole body was floating, but at other times this peculiar sensation was confined only to the legs. Occasionally I felt that I was standing on my head which was most uncomfortable. When I had these sensations, I would look at how I was lying in order to give my brain the correct information. I also used a relaxation technique; think about various parts of my body and eventually my perception – knowing where I was in time and space – became more normal.

Professor Chalker came to see me with his registrar. The professor was a short, dapper man about the same age as Peter. In some ways, he reminded me of Peter and I could understand why they were colleagues. He said that he had spoken to Peter about me and he seemed impressed. I knew that Peter would speak highly of me.

Professor Chalker went on to explain that I had fractured my spine at the first cervical vertebra (where the head joins the neck) and talked about the type of fracture. He said that I had damaged my spinal cord and I was in spinal shock. The resulting trauma and swelling of the spinal cord were affecting the nerves and how they worked. There was a possibility that I may recover my ability to breathe and some use of my arms once the swelling around the cord went down but only time would tell. Often this swelling lasted many weeks.

After he was gone, I thought about what the professor had said. It was a very high fracture, and I had been very lucky to survive the accident. I was even luckier to survive without any brain damage due to lack of oxygen thanks to the people who'd stopped to help. Obviously, I was a quadriplegic, but I desperately hoped more than anything that I would recover my ability to breathe. I did not want to live on a machine for the rest of my life. I also hoped that I would recover some use of my hands. But could I live with being in a wheelchair?

I did not know a lot about spinal injuries but had nursed a few quadriplegics. One was a man who lived in a nursing home and spent a large part of his day in bed reading. Would I end up like him and be satisfied with that sort of life? What about David? What about our marriage? *What a pity I didn't die*, I thought, *it would have been so easy.* I reflected on my near-death experience. If that is what it is like to die, then dying is very pleasant.

Later that day, Professor Nguyen asked me if I was willing to have a tracheostomy (an opening in the neck into which a tube is inserted to help with breathing). The endotracheal tube would be removed, and I would be more comfortable. Moreover, they would be able to give me a tracheostomy, which would enable me to speak with assistance. I readily agreed. He said that he would contact the neurosurgeon.

Why are all neurosurgeons tall and slim? I wondered when we met the following day. The neurosurgeon explained that he would put tongs in my head and would do the tracheostomy operation at the same time. Tongs are metal arcs which are inserted into the skull bone on either side of the head. They could probably fit me in at the end of the list on Friday but if this was not possible, then the following week. I hoped that it would be Friday because I could not tolerate the endotracheal tube much longer.

Thankfully on Friday afternoon I went to theatre and came back with the front part of my head shaved and tongs in place. Though they looked gruesome, I barely felt that the tongs were there. The tongs were attached by a string to weights which hung over the back of the bed. These weights put traction on the fracture and helped it to heal.

I also had the tracheostomy. The respirator was connected to the tube in my neck and was sticking out from the tracheostomy. My neck was a little sore where the cut had been made, but it was a relief to have that wretched endotracheal tube taken out. At last, I could swallow without it hurting. But still I could not talk because the cuff, a little balloon that fits around the tracheostomy tube, was inflated to prevent air passing through my vocal cords. One of the nurses suggested that I click with my tongue if I needed help and I soon learnt to do this.

She also explained how the Pit Speaking tube worked. This was a part of the tracheostomy tube, and the external part was connected to compressed air. This allowed air to pass above the tracheostomy and through the vocal cords thus enabling me to speak. There was a hole in the speaking tube which had to be closed in order for this to happen. David learnt to use it very quickly as did many of my visitors. Unfortunately, others did not, and communication remained difficult with them.

I soon settled into the ward routine. All the nurses introduced themselves at the start of each shift so that I would know who was looking after me. They also wore badges with an animal or flower and their name on them. This was a good idea as it helped me to remember who was who. Every morning I was washed and the bed linen was changed. When time permitted the nurses also manicured my nails and rubbed cream into my skin. The mouth toilets continued until I was able to eat, then the nurses had to brush my teeth which was a strange experience. I wore white anti-embolism stockings (elastic stockings which help prevent blood clots forming; a common complication for people who spend a long time in bed). I was also given injections of Calciparin to prevent clots forming.

'There is some advantage in being paralysed,' I remarked as I watched the nurse inject me in the leg. It was very easy to feel disassociated from my paralysed body.

I was placed on an electrically operated bed, and every two hours was turned. A nurse held my head, and the dressers worked the bed to position me. Regular turning was necessary to prevent bed sores. I had to keep my head still to keep the fracture in alignment and to prevent any further damage to my spinal cord. When I was lying flat, sandbags were placed either side of my head to keep it still. It was very hard to learn not to shake or nod my head because these are such automatic actions. At regular intervals, my temperature, pulse, respiration and blood pressure were checked and urine measured. Blood tests were taken to check the oxygen levels, my electrolyte balance and other tests were done which helped the doctors care for me. They also checked my breathing and heart rate daily and listened for bowel sounds. The neurological testing continued, but there was no response from my paralysed limbs. My sensation was tested with a pin. I had normal feeling to the base of the neck and numbed sensation in an area like a necklace below that. Lower down I felt nothing at all. It was very strange to know that my body was there, intact, but be able to feel only nothingness.

The physiotherapist worked on my chest initially twice a day and then daily. She also returned to suction me (remove secretions from my windpipe) regularly, while nurses did it at other times. I seemed to have a lot of secretions, and glad that I'd never smoked because my chest problems would have been far worse if I had. Sometimes I had plugs of mucous, and this caused me a sudden shortness of breath that was very frightening. This was relieved by hand-ventilating and suctioning me. In some ways it was a contradiction because though I did not wish to be kept alive on a respirator, I desperately fought for breath when my breathing was restricted.

Because of the physical impact of the shock of the accident my bowels had stopped working. I was, therefore, unable to eat for a couple of weeks until they started up again. My mouth felt very dry, and my tongue became furred. But it was wonderful when I was given a piece of ice to suck; it was deliciously cool and refreshing. After a few days, I was allowed to have regular ice blocks. David bought me one with blueberry and orange flavouring, but it turned my tongue black. I took great delight in showing my tongue to everyone.

Gradually the fluids were increased, and then I was allowed to eat a little soup and jelly. Once I could tolerate this the nasogastric tube was removed, which was a relief as it had been irritating my nose. Gradually I started eating a normal diet. About a week later, the nasogastric tube had to be replaced for a few days, following a bout of vomiting. This was particularly distressing as I still had to lie flat, so I was turned on my side and had the vomit removed by suctioning. I felt sorry for the nurse who was looking after me that shift.

I started to develop high temperatures, often above thirty-nine degrees Celsius and once reaching forty degrees. Bearing in mind, the normal range is between thirty-six and thirty-seven degrees. The cause of these high temperatures was sought. Sometimes a chest infection or urinary infection was found, and I was given antibiotics. At other times no infection could be found. The doctors worried that I was throwing off emboli (small blood clots which travel through the body), but again the tests were negative. I felt that it could be my body reacting to all the physical changes imposed on it. As a child, I had often had very high temperatures for no apparent reason.

After a few weeks, I realised that I would never breathe normally again. I was devastated. The thought of being kept alive on a machine for the rest of my life was almost unbearable. I thought about other people on respirators whom I had nursed. They had either recovered sufficiently to no longer need the machines or slipped deeper into a coma and brain death when the machine was turned off. I had never nursed someone like me; a thinking, rational human being. I pondered on the moral question of whether I should be kept alive on a respirator or whether the machine should be turned off and nature allowed to take its course. I was to think about this often over the next year.

The off-duty ambulance driver who had resuscitated me called by to ask how I was. I said all right and thanked him for saving my life. I hoped my words sounded sincere because I was not sure of my feelings. Often, I did wish that I'd died, but felt no animosity toward him or my other rescuers; they had done the right thing. Had I been there as a rescuer and not a victim I would have done the same. Besides, they could not have predicted the extent of the damage to my body. Slowly I started to come around to the view that having survived I had no choice but to live and to try finding some purpose in my life; to write a book about my experiences.

However, I bitterly grieved for the many losses in my life. No longer would I be able to go bushwalking and enjoy the sights and smells of the bush. No longer would I be able to go cross-country skiing and feel the crisp cold air on my cheeks or enjoy the thrill of a downhill run after a hard climb. No longer would we be able to go camping and feed the kangaroos at dusk. All the plans that David and I had to travel and cycle were dashed. I deeply regretted the impact that my accident had on his life. I also thought about work a lot. Would I be able to return to work and if so, in what capacity? Apart from periods of travel and a year at college, I had worked all my adult life. I enjoyed working and I had a strong need to help others.

What a waste, I thought, *I have all this knowledge and expertise and I can't use it. I'm sure that I can find some way of using it, I must. If I had died, all that knowledge would have been lost, and that would have been such a waste.*

Helen visited regularly and gave reports as to what was happening at work and also asked for my advice on various matters. Other colleagues both from within the team and within the area visited and kept me informed about political developments as well as social events. This all helped me to feel useful and wanted which was very important as my image of myself as a competent, caring health worker was shattered. I grieved for my loss of independence. I longed to be able to get up out of bed, and I deeply wished I could do things for myself.

I can't even scratch my bloody nose, I thought. My face itched frequently; sometimes I could let the itches go but often they drove me mad, and I had to ask someone to scratch them for me.

Being fed was particularly difficult and still is. I had never realised how much the pleasure of eating is connected to being able to feed yourself. You can select what you want to eat, in the order that you want and consume at your own pace. Lying down made it harder to swallow, and the fact that I had a pronounced gag reflex did not help either. I lost my appetite and often did not care whether I ate or not. The hospital food did not tempt me because it was rather bland – often meat and two veg. Previously I'd eaten a very varied diet with lots of fresh vegetables, rice or pasta, cheese but only a small amount of meat. The dietitian came to see me and I switched to a vegetarian diet which I preferred.

'Don't worry Hil, I'll look after you,' David pledged again.

'I don't want anyone to look after me,' I cried to myself. 'I want to be the free, independent person I always was. I want to come and go as I please, I don't want to be like this. I don't want people to care for me, not even you. I wanted us to grow old together. I wanted to care for you.'

I smiled at him and blew a kiss, knowing he was sincere.

I continued to grieve and most of all grieving for my hands. Those clever, creative hands now lying limp and useless beside me. I wished that I could knit because it would help pass the time. I had great plans to do lots more weaving when I finished my college course; now I never would. What about that bag of wool that I had been meaning to spin for months? How could I find creative ways of relaxing now? I wished that I could read a book, but I could not hold one. I found this difficult because I had always been an avid reader. David and other visitors read to me which I enjoyed, but they felt self-conscious.

One of the nurses asked the occupational therapist to see me. She placed two straps on the mirror above my bed which was good for reading books, but magazines tended to fall down. Later she bought a Perspex stand and a book could be placed on top of this so I could read them. This was better, but I needed someone to turn the pages. This was fine if the ward was quiet but not worth asking when they were busy. I found it difficult to occupy my time and listened to the radio a lot and played tapes.

What hurt the most was my inability to reach out and touch a fellow human being. To be able to take someone's hand, to be able to hug a child and tousle its hair - how I longed to do that. I wished desperately to put my arms around David and to caress his cheek. I missed the physical side of our relationship; not only our sexual relationship but also the caresses, holding hands, sleeping beside him and knowing that he was there. It was to be like an empty ache the whole time I was in hospital. Our private lives had suddenly become very public. Gone were the quiet times together which we valued so much. All this put a very considerable strain on our relationship.

Then I thought about home. Would I ever see my house again? It was a small Victorian semi-detached house with a long narrow hallway and two steps between the hall and the lounge room. It would be impossible to make it wheelchair accessible. Could I go home anyway? Would I have to live in a nursing home or an institution for people with disabilities? I dreaded the thought. *What about David and what about our marriage?* I thought, *what sort of life would I have at home anyway?*

I looked at the respirator. Would I continue to need oxygen? That would be very costly especially if I also needed compressed air to talk. I imagined myself at home connected to two large cylinders.

It is ironic, I thought, *that I have spent all these years doing counselling courses and attending seminars so that I could improve my communication skills and teach others to improve theirs. Now I'm dependent on a piece of tubing and someone to help me in order to talk.* I felt depressed. Would I ever talk again? One of nurses told me about Paul who was also a ventilator-dependent quadriplegic. Apparently, he had learnt to talk properly. I wondered how he did it and felt a glimmer of hope.

I worried about our cat because on previous occasions when I had been away, he had pined for me. He wandered around the house looking lost or sat outside the bedroom door. He also went off his food. David admitted that was how he was behaving now. How I wished that I could have him on the bed and stroke his soft fur and listen to his loud purr. I knew that he would forget me in time and I felt sad. All these thoughts and many others went around and around in my head.

I knew that it was normal to grieve and to experience feelings of shock, denial, anger, *why me?*, depression, bargaining and acceptance. I recovered from the shock of the accident fairly quickly. Partly because of my prior knowledge as a nurse, I was able to piece together what was happening and believe that I was paralysed. However, in the two areas which mattered to me most, breathing and being able to use my hands, I kept hoping for improvement. Often, I thought that I had feeling in my upper arms, but neurological testing showed that this was not so. This denial is a normal defence mechanism which we use when the impact of what has happened is too great to believe and accept. Though I had moments of anger, these did not last long. Nor was my anger directed against anyone, which it might have been had my accident been caused by someone else. I did bargain to regain my breathing and use of my hands. That is, if I did regain these, I would do my utmost to use my hands and voice in the best ways possible.

Because my accident was unforeseen and unpreventable and was purely an accident, I did not ask *why me?* I have no religious beliefs and therefore did not believe as some people do that God was punishing me. Also, I find the belief that people are punished through accident or illness totally unacceptable, but this did not stop me having periods of depression and cried frequently. I accepted that I was paralysed and eventually that I would not breathe again for myself. But I did not go beyond this at that time probably because there were too many unknown factors. At first, it was difficult for me to accept help, but after a while, I felt comfortable with people caring for me and attending to all my physical needs.

How did I cope with all this? I talked to David, family and friends and to the nurses who were very supportive. I cried and found release in my tears, and I practised relaxation; a technique which I had used for some years. A colleague gave me a tape on valuing yourself, and I played this when I went to sleep at night and during very down moments. All this helped me to cope with the sudden and immense changes in my life.

From the first days, cards and flowers arrived in such numbers that my bed bay took on the appearance of a cross between a florist and a stationer's. A friend had Mass said for me and many friends prayed for me. I also had visits from friends and colleagues who often arrived looking concerned, not knowing what to say. Many people asked if they could do things for me. My initial reaction was to say, 'No, I'm all right thanks.' Obviously, I was not. I decided that as I needed help and that it would also help my visitors feel less inadequate, I would accept their help. All this concern and caring helped me through this very difficult period.

I thought, *if I'd died, I would have had a good funeral. Poor David, it would have been hard on him. In time he would have been able to live without me, but he would have been very lonely. Hopefully, in time, he would meet someone else.*

My mother Molly came down from Queensland where she lived and stayed with David. My father did not come because he was confined to a wheelchair due to polio and his disability had worsened as he grew older. I was, of course, very happy to see my mother, though I wish that the circumstances were different. She spent most of the day with me but unfortunately, she did not feel comfortable using the speaking tube, so we had to devise other ways of communicating. Lip reading was all right up to a point but quickly became frustrating when I was not understood. My mother wrote words and sentences on a piece of board and I would click when she pointed to the right word; we used this as a method of communication. However, this was very slow and restricted our conversation. If only I could write.

I saw my eldest brother and his wife regularly as they lived in Canberra and visited her elderly parents in Sydney. My sister-in-law had a natural talent for lip reading and we rarely resorted to using the speaking tube. My nephew, however, quickly became bored like many young boys and when bored he fidgeted. This made us all nervous because of the machinery, knobs and dials about. Consequently, they often cut their visits short. My youngest brother arrived from Adelaide, tall and gangly despite his thirty-three years. We both felt awkward and did not know what to say. He read poetry to me and gave me a pair of headphones which I used for a while until they fell apart.

About a month after my accident when the other family members had returned home, my sister arrived from England. It was so good to see her. Gill and I were very close, and we always regretted that we lived so far apart. I had seen her two years previously on our last trip to Europe, but Gill had not visited Australia for over twenty years. She had been planning a visit sometime in the not too distant future, and I had thought about some of the places we could go to and some of the things we could do together. I did not want it to be like this. All the same, I was thrilled to see her. She spent most of her time with me, and we talked and laughed together. She bought face lotions and gave me facial massages which were very relaxing. She read to me and generally endeavoured to keep me amused. I also enjoyed being fed by her, probably because we had similar eating habits and I stopped losing weight while she was around. I missed her desperately when she went home, but I realised that she had family and job commitments to return to. If anything happened to David, I decided, I would endeavour to move to England so that we could see each other often. She had also been a good support to David as he found her easy to talk to.

The only other member of my family whom I did not see was my second brother who lived in Darwin. He had married recently and was not financially well off. I had planned to visit him and his wife with David either that year or the next. He kept in frequent contact with my mother. I knew too that he found it very hard to come to terms with my disability because we had also been very close.

In April I had my forty-fourth birthday but did not want to celebrate. David and I had planned to go to Melbourne, stay in a small hotel and have dinner at a top restaurant, then go on to Castlemaine and spend the weekend at a bicycle rally. No, I did not want to celebrate my birthday. I wanted to hibernate, hoping the day would pass as quickly as possible. But it was not to be. David arrived with streamers and balloons with which he festooned my bed. He also brought a plastic, blow-up birthday cake complete with candles which Gill had sent to him especially for the occasion. After a breakfast of croissants, he left and went to work. Numerous friends came during the day. Helen and other colleagues from work bought birthday cakes which we shared around. Later in the evening the nurses gathered around my bed and sang Happy Birthday.

Two Intensive Care

They opened a bottle of champagne, and I had a small glass. It had been a good day after all, and I was deeply touched by everyone's kindness.

Time weighed very heavily on my hands. I had gone from a very busy active lifestyle to being unable to do anything for myself. The days stretched ahead of me, grey and empty. How was I to keep occupied? Then David bought me a Walkman radio, and every morning I listened to music and talkback shows on the radio. It became my lifeline as it kept me in touch with the world outside the hospital as well as keeping me amused. In the afternoon I played tapes and watched television. However, I found all these passive activities stifling and boredom continued to be a problem the whole time that I was in hospital. It was always a relief to have someone to talk to as it helped pass the time. I was also pleased when I could read or be read to. I asked David to bring in my watch so I could keep track of the time. Sometimes I could not sleep at night and would lie awake thinking, listening to music or practising relaxation. Intensive Care was noisy because of the numerous machines and sick patients I started taking sleeping tablets and slept better; waking only for turns and observations.

I started to lose weight again. However, I was pleased about this because I had been overweight, and I knew that it would be much easier to care for me if I were many kilograms lighter. The other pleasing thing was that I never felt hungry. I thought about the times that I had tried to diet unsuccessfully. I had always been hungry. After some weeks my body became quite oedematous; meaning I had fluid in the tissues. Blood tests showed that I had low protein and low sodium. At the time I could not understand this as I thought I was eating as much protein and more salt than prior to my accident. The loss of protein could possibly have been explained by the extra physical demands on my body by infections, poor appetite and weight loss.

The dietitian saw me again, and I agreed to take protein supplements and to eat chicken and fish. Unfortunately, I frequently had baked fish served to me which was often dry and tasteless, sometimes three or four days running. Attempts to rectify this situation were unsuccessful, and in the end, I switched from the mainly vegetarian diet to a ward diet so that I could choose what I wanted. I never ever chose baked fish again.

To rectify the low sodium I took salt tablets, initially one three times a day but increasing to four tablets three times a day as the problem persisted. I hated them. No matter how fast I swallowed, they left an aftertaste. I found that eating jellybeans took this taste away, but I felt a bit like a young child who is given a lolly for being good. The other side effect which was more distressing was that it made my tears very salty. Every time I cried my eyes stung unbearably and had to ask for them to be wiped away. This remained a problem long after I ceased taking the tablets.

Though I had been in hospital many weeks now, I had never asked anyone to clean my ears. Then over the period of about a week, I became increasingly deaf. Though I complained about my lack of hearing to the nurses, I did not ask the doctors to look in my ears to see what was happening. Then one morning I woke up and I could hear nothing at all.

Am I to be deaf as well as mute? I thought, *how in the hell am I to communicate now? I can't write. What will I do with myself? I can't hear the radio. What else can go wrong?*

The doctors examined my ears and found that they were full of wax. I was surprised as this had never been a problem before. I'd occasionally cleaned my ears with a cotton bud, but that was all. The doctors were concerned that one of the antibiotics I had taken had affected my hearing. The same thought crossed my mind and I hoped that I would not be permanently deaf. The doctors arranged to syringe my ears which was difficult as I was still lying flat in bed and I was not supposed to turn my head. I had my ears syringed three times at weekly intervals and thankfully my hearing improved.

Following the last syringing, my ears popped and whooshed as they gradually cleared. I was seen by an Ear, Nose and Throat specialist who advised that my hearing would improve when I was finally able to be sat up and moved around. This proved to be correct. Following the first syringing, ear drops were prescribed to soften the wax and again these were difficult to put in because I could not turn my head.

Communication was difficult for about two months, and during this time it was me who had to lip read. With some people this was easy, but with others far from it. I asked people to shout which was embarrassing for them especially while I was still in Intensive Care. Our conversations were hardly private. I could not listen to the radio for about three days; then I was just able to hear by turning the volume up to the highest setting. As my ears started to clear, I had to ask for frequent adjustment to the volume as my hearing fluctuated between being almost normal to hearing very little. It was a great relief when my hearing fully returned.

When I was admitted to Intensive Care, I had noticed the social worker talking to other patients and I wondered when she would come to me. I would have liked to talk to her about my concerns about work and the future. Eventually, she approached the end of my bed and nervously asked how I was. I wondered whether she thought I had AIDS or something. The nurse offered to show her how to use the speaking tube, but she mumbled some excuse and fluttered off. I was disappointed. Later when this social worker interviewed David, I was annoyed. *She can talk to him because it is easy, but she can't be bothered making the effort of learning to talk to me. I'm the one who had the accident. Does she think I'm non-compos?* I thought crossly. I also made my views clear to one of the nurses. I felt somewhat mollified when David said that their conversation was not particularly helpful. From then on, I dismissed the social worker as ineffectual and regarded her tentative inquiries as to my health as intrusions on my privacy.

How different to the social workers who had worked with my rehabilitation team, I reflected. Unfortunately, our current social worker was in Europe on a year's leave without pay.

After I had been in hospital a month, David was interviewed by the spinal injuries' social worker about our eligibility for assistance from the Provision of Aids for Disabled Persons scheme. The PADP is a government-funded scheme that provides aids and equipment to people with disabilities. But like many, such funding is limited, and an assessment of a person's financial status is necessary. I was on the PADP committee in the area in which I worked and therefore was very familiar with its functions.

Because David was being asked about our personal finances, I felt that this time it was appropriate that he talk to the social worker privately. I worried that we would not fit the eligibility criteria because we were both professional working people at the time of my accident. However, David had made the decision to give up work to care for me. We would live on my invalid pension and though it entailed a dramatic change to our lifestyle and financial status we felt that this was the best solution. Because we were buying the house, we did not have a large amount of savings. It was a relief when David came back and said that he had been advised that we did fit the criteria.

Two weeks later David had an interview with Professor Chalker. He returned from the interview with a face like thunder. Something was terribly wrong, and I felt frightened. It took David a while before he calmed down sufficiently to tell me.

'Professor Chalker says that we are both professional

people and earning too much money. We have to pay for the ventilator ourselves. It costs fourteen and a half thousand dollars. We will have to sell the house.'

I was shocked and horrified. What was the point of the social work assessment? We were, after all, eligible for PADP funding. The accident had happened on a Sunday morning, and no other vehicle was involved. Therefore, I was not covered by any insurance. But if the house was sold, where would we live? Were all those years of hard work and stinting to pay off mortgages to be for nothing? But it was not just the ventilator; there was all the other equipment that I would need. An electric wheelchair, for instance, cost several thousand dollars. What else would we have to sell? Was it not enough that we had to give up our jobs? Perhaps David and I should get a divorce and then I would be eligible.

It was all too much, and I cried inconsolably. *I hate myself*, I thought, *I don't want to be like this, I'm so bloody useless. I don't want to live on a machine. It's not fair. It's not fair for me or David. Just when the future was looking good and now this.*

We were both very angry and upset. We talked to the Intensive Care staff and to friends, and they all expressed surprise. Professor Nguyen tried to reassure us and said that we would be funded and supplied with a ventilator. However, I continued to have nagging doubts. We felt trapped and desperate; the reality of our situation had hit us hard. David and Helen bought Lotto tickets. If only we could win a million dollars, but we never did.

What cost a human life? I pondered later when we had calmed down. *Fourteen and a half thousand dollars. That's a lot of money. Is my life worth that much?* I thought about the Community Health Services. *We could run some good programs with that money and help a lot of people. And what about the third world? We could help thousands; vaccination programmes and build new wells. Who is to say that my life is worth more than theirs? We have this belief in the west that it is life at any cost, but it is the quality of life that matters. A heart transplant would cost more and what about liver transplants? It's the sort of thing people argue about for years. It is all too difficult,* I decided. *All I know is that having survived the accident, I have no choice but to live and make the best of it. Unfortunately, that means supplying me with a lot of expensive equipment.*

Another matter which was to occupy our minds at that time and for the next few months was the question of care. I had very high dependency needs because I was physically unable to do anything for myself. I was familiar with community nursing services having worked for one myself for several years. I knew that they would only be able to come for about an hour each morning to attend to my personal care and any dressings. I was also familiar with the home care services which provided a personal care attendant for longer periods during the day but again hours were restricted plus they'd sent an attendant who the coordinator thought was suitable. However, I had heard of another scheme whereby the disabled person employs their own attendants but unfortunately did not know the name of this scheme.

Initially, David could not understand why I wanted carers because wasn't he going to look after me? I had seen too many carers who felt that they had to manage on their own either because they did not know about the services available or because they felt it was their duty. All too often they either became ill or burnt out. I was determined that this was not going to happen to David. He was too precious to me.

We started to make enquiries. We asked the social worker, people with my team and other teams within the area. There were costly private schemes, but no one seemed to know of the scheme I was talking about. I felt totally frustrated. If only I could use the phone. A colleague of David's said that his wife could help as she was a social worker. He was very upset when a week later he received a scrappy note giving us less information than we had already with a suggestion that we talk to the occupational therapists.

It was not until I had been in hospital for five months and I mentioned the problem to a friend and colleague of mine, Sue, that we finally resolved the problem. She spoke with Sarah, the social worker on her team. Sarah came to see me and explained about the "3-2-5" bed scheme. An application had to be made on my behalf through an organisation such as Paraquad to the Commonwealth Health Service in Canberra. It usually took about three months to process. The advantage of the scheme was that I could employ my own attendants and once approved the funding would be transferred to wherever I chose to live. The maximum number of hours was thirty-five hours per week. It was as though a great weight had been lifted off me. I could not wait to tell David and show him the information that Sarah had left with me.

David, however, was so fed up with the whole business that he was not ready to listen, so he shouted at me and stormed off. Fortunately, with my permission, Sarah had talked with the spinal unit social worker. He contacted Paraquad and put a submission together. He came to see David and me, and we talked about our needs and the number of hours required. We decided that we needed twenty-eight hours of attendant care, preferably someone with nursing experience but not necessarily formal training and seven hours of nursing care. After I had read the final submission, it was sent to Canberra.

Good, I thought, *at least that will be there by the time I am ready to go home.*

After two months I became very restless and impatient. I no longer felt unwell and I was anxious to get moving and try and pick up the threads of my life. I was fed up with lying in bed, but I still had the tongs in place because the fracture had not healed. There were only small high windows in the Intensive Care unit, and I longed to get out of hospital to see the trees and the sky and to hear the birds sing. I felt that I was wasting my life. I was frustrated by my physical disability and wished yet again that I could use my hands. I also became impatient for things to happen. I had been told that I would be going to the spinal injuries ward, but I could not be transferred until Paul (another ventilator-dependent quadriplegic) was discharged. There seemed to be frequent delays in his discharge. I knew that he had been in hospital well over a year and had a lot of lung problems.

What's wrong with the guy? Doesn't he want to go home? I thought crossly and wondered whether he had been in hospital too long. Often when people stay in hospital for long periods, they become institutionalised. In other words, they feel so comfortable and secure with the routine, the care and the lack of day to day worries, that they are reluctant to leave. However, I was unaware that Paul was having a very frustrating time waiting for his electric wheelchair to arrive.

Paul and his wife Penny came to see me before he went home. I looked at him, a fairly tall man sitting in an electric wheelchair with a chin control. He had a tracheostomy with thick tubing connecting him to the ventilator. The ventilator was like a large metal box which was placed on the back of the chair. Paul also talked quite volubly, though I noticed that Penny carried a syringe so that she could pump-up the cuff of Paul's tracheostomy if he ran short of air. I thought, *that is how I will look to other people.* Both Paul and Penny were very encouraging and left saying that they would see us again.

All these hassles affected our relationship and David and I started to bicker and fight. It was usually over little things such as the way I ate. Because I was lying flat, I often found it difficult to swallow and needed to drink frequently. I also took smaller mouthfuls and ate more slowly than he did. But for David, who was hungry after having had a long day at work, it was all extremely irritating.

In the past, we had usually talked over problems between us, but now I wished that he had someone else to talk to. I found it difficult to cope with my own stress, let alone with his. I thought again of the team social worker; she was a friend as well as a colleague. I knew that he could talk to her, but unfortunately, she was so far away.

Why do we fight with the person that we are closest to? Often it is due to the stress of the situation. We are both more sensitive to what is said and therefore more likely to react negatively. Also, because the person cares for you and you are fairly certain that they will return tomorrow, it is safe to be angry with them. Sometimes this anger is deflected. For example, people in hospital often feel angry with doctors or nurses, but because they are a patient, they feel it's inappropriate to express their anger toward them. So instead they become angry with the person they love most.

After two months I was no longer an acutely ill patient; therefore, nurses were assigned to someone else other than to me. Often because other patients were sicker than me, their needs came first. I tried to be patient, but at times it was very difficult. David said that I was very demanding and one of the nurses obviously thought so too. I called her Miss Bossy Boots. Our conversations went something like this:

I would click for attention. She would answer, 'It will have to wait, Hilary. Can't you see we're busy?'

'All right, Miss Bossy Boots,' I would say to myself but not entirely convinced.

Yet at other times she was very caring, though one of the other nurses did disturb me as she had rather strange views which she felt that I should share. As I was unable to communicate in the normal manner, I found this rather frightening. Fortunately, the nursing unit manager had previously advised me that if I did feel uncomfortable with any of the nurses, I was to tell her and that nurse would be assigned elsewhere. But I felt reluctant to do this. On balance I liked most of the nurses, and some were like good friends. I looked forward to the next time that they would be caring for me.

It made no difference to me as to whether the nurse was male or female as I regarded male nurses as much a part of the nursing profession as female doctors are a part of the medical profession. I hope in time people will stop worrying about a person's gender and look to their skills and expertise.

Nor did I worry about the numerous people who examined, treated or washed my body. I had long ago lost any inhibitions about my body through frequent camping and walking trips. Besides, mine was not the sort of body most people would find excessively attractive. Being a health worker myself I also knew that health workers rarely regard their patients in a sexual way but rather with clinical detachment. I did, however, object to being exposed to other patients or their relatives and vice-versa. I found it embarrassing and they did too.

Only with hindsight, I realise how angry I was during this

period. However, at the time I was only in touch with my frustrations and the apparent lack of progress. Finally, at the end of three months, the tongs were removed. This was done on the ward and they came out easily. At last some progress.

The next day Paul went home, and I was transferred to the spinal unit. I was pleased but apprehensive.

Three
Spinal Injuries Unit

'The journey of a thousand miles starts with a single step.'
Chinese proverb

I seemed to have quite an entourage when I moved to the spinal ward. I was lifted onto a trolley and connected to a small portable respirator. Two nurses accompanied me plus Denis, the spinal injury's registrar, who had seen me several times in Intensive Care and Colin, the technician. The other nurses said goodbye and wished me well. Outside it was a bright sunny day, and for the first time in three months, I could see blue sky and trees. I enjoyed every minute of the push up the hill to the spinal ward which was housed in a low white building near the front of the hospital. I was wheeled into the acute end of the ward and transferred onto another bed. To my disappointment the windows were small and high up, but I could see some sky.

I was changed over onto another respirator and Colin fiddled with the controls until I was comfortable. It is hard to describe how it feels being switched from one respirator to another. Normally you never think about the way you breathe, but it is like being asked to breathe in a different manner to the way you are accustomed. For a few minutes you are very conscious of it then it becomes a part of you. This respirator was fairly noisy, but I soon got used to the sound except when the battery alarm went off. This seemed to happen regularly in the middle of the night. As the battery worked the other alarms, it could not be turned off. Colin tried to rectify this situation by changing the batteries during the day.

Whilst in Intensive Care I had been on oxygen that had been gradually reduced and continued to be reduced in the ward until no longer needed. This was a huge relief and visions of me sitting at home surrounded by explosive oxygen cylinders vanished. But I still needed compressed air for the speaker tube to enable me to talk. This meant that someone had to collect a cylinder of air and place it by my bed. Sometimes the air ran out, and I would spend a frustrating time unable to speak to visitors until the next cylinder arrived. I also disliked the tubing being placed near my ears. *Shh huh* went the respirator in my right ear, *sshhh* went the air in my left ear. It drove me crazy and I repeatedly asked for the tubing to be moved. One of the nurses stuck the air tubing near her ear.

'Oh, I think it's quite sexy,' as she offered it to one of the dressers.

We all laughed.

Though I'd wanted to move to the spinal unit because it was the next step in my recovery, I was very uptight.

'What's wrong with you?' David said in exasperation. 'I thought you wanted to come up here.'

'Leave me alone,' I replied.

One of the nurses explained that it was usual for people to feel anxious when being transferred from Intensive Care to a ward. I was anxious for a number of reasons. I had been used to one nurse caring for me and one other patient only. The ratio on this ward was two nurses caring for six patients. Would they hear me when I clicked for help? Would they understand what I wanted? Could they and would they use the speaker tube? Were these nurses as nice as the ones in Intensive Care? Would they expect me to do things which I could not do? Would they do the things I asked? My anxiety lessened after a few days as I quickly realised that the nurse would hear me when I clicked and as I came to know them individually. Most cared for me well and tried to comply with my requests. Maureen, for example, always ensured that I was positioned correctly, that I was comfortable and that I had something to do. This was very important to me as boredom and having too much time to think were my biggest problems. There were two nurses however, who consistently left me lying on my back staring at the ceiling without my radio. This used to anger me.

'I've spent three bloody months staring at the ceiling,' I swore to myself. 'Yes, it is damn boring. Do you think it's all right to leave me lying here like this? Don't you think that I have needs? Do you think I don't count?'

This came to a head one day when one of the pairs dashed off to attend to a new admission. One of the aides entered the ward and I clicked to gain her attention. The nurse was furious and came up to my bed.

'How dare you click!' she stormed. 'Can't you see we're busy. You're not the only patient in here.'

'I wasn't clicking you,' I retorted. 'I was trying to get the attention of the aide.'

'Who the hell do you think you are?' came the response. 'You're not the only one here.'

She later apologised but I was surprised at how upset she was. I could see her viewpoint that I was making trivial demands when they were busy with an important admission and should have waited. I reiterated what I had said about the aide and explained that I was bored. Had I been able to talk properly I would have called out to the aide, but I was still reliant on the speaker tube.

Many of the nurses were good lip readers and only used the tube for difficult sentences. Others used the tube most of the time, and others did neither. This quickly became very frustrating as I repeated myself for the tenth time to someone who still could not lip read what I had said. I decided that I would only repeat myself three times and then insist that the other person use the speaker tube. Unfortunately, I reduced one of the student nurses to tears one night because she had not been shown how to use the speaker tube and could not understand what I was saying.

I became increasingly frustrated by my inability to speak clearly. Conversation was limited mostly to basic requests. Even with David and my friends, I was frustrated by being unable to join in conversations freely and sometimes people would talk over the top of me. Nor could I join in the ward conversation, be part of the repartee between the staff and patients. I felt increasingly miserable and left out; of becoming a non-person.

Then, almost as if he had read my mind, Professor Nguyen came to see me. He explained how I could learn to talk by partially letting down the tracheostomy cuff and then squeezing my glottis to prevent too much air escaping. The glottis is a small muscle at the back of the hard palate in the mouth which closes off the trachea when we swallow. Letting down the tracheostomy cuff allowed air to pass through my vocal cords and I could speak.

We practised for a minute while he was there. I felt apprehensive and breathless but managed to say a few words. Following that, I practised with Lorrain, the head physiotherapist who did my morning therapy. It was a slow process, but gradually I was able to speak for five minutes, then fifteen, then half an hour. I exchanged jokes with the physiotherapists during these sessions.

I also practised with David when he visited in the evening. Maureen was quite happy to show him how to deflate the cuff because she was accustomed to Paul's care, but some of the other nurses were clearly alarmed at the idea. I seemed to remain at the half-hour length of speaking for some weeks and always felt tired and breathless at the end of these sessions. Lorrain, after speaking to Professor Nguyen, suggested that the tidal volume (the amount of air I received with each breath) be turned up. This worked well, and I was able to increase the length and the number of times that I talked. I started asking visitors and the nurses to let my cuff down more often so that I could talk to them.

After a few weeks, my own ventilator arrived, and Karl connected me up and explained how it worked. It was a portable ventilator about the size of a small suitcase, which ran on room air and electricity. On the front were dials which showed my breathing rate and the battery charge level. There were various alarm buttons such as low pressure which usually meant that the tubing had become disconnected and a high-pressure alarm which usually meant that I needed suctioning. These alarms could be turned off by pressing a reset button. A panel at the front opened to reveal more controls which Karl set to my individual breathing needs. The ventilator could be plugged into the mains electricity or run off a battery and had its own internal battery which lasted forty-five minutes. I was pleased and relieved to receive it because I had continued to have nagging doubts about the funding. Now I would be free to move around. Progress at last.

I decided to stop taking the sleeping tablets as I seemed to be sleeping a lot during the day as well as at night. I sometimes left with a hangover-like feeling. Besides that, I felt it preferable not to take any medication unless I really had to. I reduced the tablets gradually so that I did not have any side effects such as sleepless nights, disturbed dreams and restlessness. After a month I stopped taking them altogether. There were some nights when I slept very little, but I no longer worried about this and was happy to lie awake thinking or practising relaxation.

As soon as my bowels had started to work again, the nurses had started a regime of laxatives every other day and an enema the following morning. I always pitied the nurses who had to clean me up because as a nurse I had never found it a pleasant job. I tried to detach myself from what the nurses were doing and think of more pleasant things. Sometimes I had accidents during the day which initially I found embarrassing and distressing but later came to accept, as I had no control over my bowels. In the ward, the nurses were worried that I was constipated and increased my bowel care to daily. After five days I felt exhausted and quite physically ill and refused this daily treatment. Other laxatives were tried until the right regime was found.

After I had been in the ward some weeks, Denis approached me and asked whether I would consider having a suprapubic catheter inserted. Since my accident, I had a catheter which drained urine from my bladder via the urethra. A suprapubic catheter is placed through the wall of the abdomen into the bladder. The advantage of this type of catheter is that it lessens the risk of infection. There is no risk of developing a fistula (a passage) between the urethra and vagina and it enhances sexual relations.

But did I want another hole in my body? How would David feel about it? He said that it was my decision. I thought about it, the advantages clearly outweighed the disadvantages and I decided to have it done.

Denis made the arrangements, and a week later I was placed on a trolley and wheeled down to the urology theatre which was approached through a maze of narrow corridors. One of the nurses came along to look after me and the ventilator. I was given a light anaesthetic and woke up with a suprapubic catheter in place. I enjoyed a brief chat with the recovery sisters before returning to the ward. Again, it was a lovely sunny day and I enjoyed the feel of the sun on my skin.

Later Helen bought lunch that day; smoked salmon, prawns, caviar, French bread and a small bottle of champagne (Moet). It was to be the first of many such lunches. I slept well that night.

I continued to experience strange sensations. I had what I called a hypotensive feeling like a hot and cold tingling in my lower limbs most of the time. If I was feverish or otherwise disturbed such as when I had bowel care, this feeling used to creep up my body. If it reached my shoulders it became unbearable. My imaginary hands still felt twisted and knotted but had a more normal shape. Also if I closed my eyes, I could imagine straightening out my fingers until I could eventually relax them all together. I sometimes felt that I could feel parts of my body such as my back or my legs but knew that it was just in my mind playing tricks. However, I did feel hunger and nausea at the appropriate times; all very strange.

'Hello sexy,' said one of the dressers.

I looked at him in surprise. I realised that it had been said in a joking manner in order to make me laugh. I looked down at my skinny arms and flaccid bloated body. Would anyone find me sexy? I knew from the way in which David kissed me sometimes that I was still sexually attractive to him. How I wished I could caress his face and put my arms around him. How wonderful it would be to share a bed with him, just to know that he was sleeping beside me. I felt a terrible emptiness. I remember the quadriplegic man I had nursed; he said that most sexual feelings were in the mind. I wondered whether he was right.

I continued to grieve for the losses in my life and had some very down moments. The nurses were very supportive and some I found easy to talk to, but others not so. In my experience, this is normal as we all relate better to some people than to others. Some of the younger nurses did not know what to say but always held my hand or stroked my head. While I cried, this was a great comfort. Often nurses offered to draw the curtains around me so that I could have some privacy, but I usually declined because I did not like the closed in feeling.

David and I were still trying to sort out our lives. We had

decided to sell our house because it was a small Victorian semi-detached and impossible to make it wheelchair accessible. I had never thought that when I rode out on that Sunday morning, I would never see my place ever again.

'It is only a house,' reasoned David. 'It is not a home without you there. It is very lonely sometimes.'

Poor man, I thought, *does not have much of a life. All day at work then he rushes over here to visit me and then goes home to an empty house.*

We decided to repaint the hallway and lounge room before selling and David started the arduous job of stripping the wallpaper. Helen and I tried to persuade him to accept help, but he wanted to do it all himself. I felt so useless.

Work was another consideration, could I return to work as team leader? Helen felt I could. I knew I could do the administrative work, the counselling and teaching once my speech improved, but what about the nursing duties such as home visits and clinics? That would be impossible. Would I now be able to cope with the physical demands of the job? I would have to return to work part-time. Perhaps I could share my time with different people and work in an administrative/advisory capacity. What would I need in order to work? A hands-free phone, a computer, a page-turning device for reading, and a secretary/attendant. That would cost a lot of money. Would my employers think that I was I worth that much? I needed to do something useful with my life. I daydreamed and imagined myself working. It was not going to be easy.

David's boss wanted him to remain at work full-time. He had a good job with good career prospects, and it would be a shame to give it away. We both felt torn between a desire to start a new life together but also for David to follow his career path. Was it possible? Much depended on my receiving enough hours of care. We felt increasingly frustrated by the difficulty in getting sufficient care once I left hospital. No matter how we tried to calculate the hours, there would just not be enough for David to work full-time. This meant that we would have to employ people privately which was very costly. Also, if we remained in Sydney, we would have to buy another house and take out a larger mortgage.

After doing our sums, we found that we would have barely enough to live on. Was it worth it? I felt such a burden on David. Why did we have to make all these difficult decisions? If only I had not had the accident. If only I were less physically disabled. If only I could look after myself just a little. If only I was paraplegic instead of quadriplegic, I could be relatively independent, needing far less care. If I had died instead of living, I would not be putting David through all this. I felt so guilty.

Poor David, I thought, *his first wife Susan had suffered from mental illness and now he has a wife who is physically disabled. How unlucky can you be? I only hope that I don't live too long and that he meets someone with whom to share an active old age. Then he can travel and do all the things we planned to do.*

Since the accident, my neck had been x-rayed regularly for signs of the fracture healing. Once there was sufficient cartilaginous tissue (scar tissue) starting to form the tongs had been removed and I was fitted with a brace. The purpose of a brace is to support the newly healed fracture whilst the patient sits up. Normally the orthotists mould the foam to the front of the patient's body after first heating the mould in a special oven. Once the front is moulded, they then fit the back of the brace and straps. In my case the front could not be moulded to my body because of the tracheostomy. I noticed one of the hospital staff walking around my bed and so asked the nurse who he was. She explained that he was the orthotist who would measure me for a brace. I expected him to measure me with a tape measure but to my surprise, he did not.

After a few days, the brace arrived and was put on. It was the most uncomfortable thing that I had ever worn because it fitted where it touched. To wear it properly, I felt that even with the straps adjusted my neck was being stretched up and back. Furthermore, it restricted my breathing and made it extremely difficult to eat or drink. I could only tolerate the brace if I slid down inside it a bit, like a tortoise in its shell. The nurses also found that the hole made for the tracheostomy was both too narrow and too high up which meant that the brace could not be pulled down properly. Some of these problems were rectified, but the brace remained uncomfortable. I persevered with it for several weeks but then started to complain at length. Not everyone was sympathetic.

'Well you broke your bloody neck,' said one of the dressers.

'You arrogant bastard,' I seethed. 'No one deliberately breaks their neck.'

But later this set me thinking once more about my accident. Was there anything I could have done to prevent it? I decided not.

Maureen contacted the head orthotist on his return from holiday and he offered to make a new brace. She also discussed the problem of my brace with Denis and Dr Angelis who was caring for me while Professor Chalker was away. After more x-rays were taken and discussions between the doctors and the orthotist, I was fitted with a semi-hard collar. It was reasonably comfortable and the relief of not having to wear the old brace immeasurable. I was very happy.

Once the new brace had been fitted, I was allowed to sit up. It was four months since my accident. At first, I sat up gradually in bed a little more each day and for longer and longer periods. Then I had my first experience of sitting out of bed. Two dressers lifted me into a wheelchair while a nurse held the ventilator tubing. But I could only tolerate about ten minutes of this because I felt terrible, weak, light-headed and nauseous. Maureen had warned me that this might be a problem, but I was still disappointed that I could not tolerate sitting up for longer.

This now became a part of my daily routine. Each day I would sit out of bed keeping my eyes firmly fixed to a painting of little birds on the wall opposite, trying and control the feelings of light-headedness and blurred vision. Often the hot and cold hypotensive feeling would creep up my body until it became unbearable or I would be overwhelmed by feelings of nausea. At these times I would ask to be put back to bed. Usually the dressers complied promptly, but a couple of them felt that I could wait. This angered both the nurses and myself, and I became very distressed. Other dressers treated me as though I was someone special and, though it could be argued that they were just doing their job, it helped me feel comfortable about asking for assistance.

Very slowly I increased my tolerance of sitting up from five minutes to half an hour but then seemed to get stuck at that level. Nausea remained the biggest problem and sometimes I needed injections to counteract it. Maureen suggested that I wear an abdominal binder (rather like an elastic corset) and I found this helped a great deal. I was then able to increase my sitting time to forty minutes, then an hour. However, eventually the binder started to make me feel worse and I dispensed with it all together. I occasionally felt dizzy, especially when first getting out of bed but this was usually transient, lasting only five or ten minutes. But if it persisted, I would ask the nurses to recline my chair to rectify the problem.

I didn't experience prolonged or frequent periods of dizziness nor did I black out which can be major issues for people with quadriplegia. But I did find it difficult to talk to groups of visitors during these periods because the constant shifting from one face to another increased my symptoms. I would ask people to sit facing me and occasionally ask them to leave. Fortunately, most understood.

I persisted with the daily routine of sitting out of bed even though it was an ordeal and I felt increasingly anxious as the time approached to get up. I wanted to progress, to be able to spend the day in a wheelchair rather than in bed. After several weeks I achieved this aim but could not sit entirely upright in the chair. The other problem was the inability to maintain my posture. I continually flopped to one side (usually the right) despite being supported by cushions. It was and still is very annoying.

During my time in Intensive Care I'd taken very little notice of the other patients, but now I did. Rick was a big Maori guy whose spine was injured when a rugby scrum collapsed. He had been in the bed opposite me. But apart from remarking on his sheepskin boots which we all wore to prevent pressure sores, I had not taken much notice of him. When I did and we would send messages to each other via David. Rick would tell the nurses when I clicked for help. I tried to offer him support and encouragement as he was going through a very rough time. I asked Helen to talk to Rick about learning relaxation as he expressed an interest. I also mentioned this to Maureen who made arrangements for the psychologist to see him.

After we had been in the ward a couple of weeks, Ossie, an abalone diver, was admitted following a car accident. He had to have his moustache shaved off so that the oxygen mask would fit properly. He had a wife and two little girls. I felt sorry for all of them and the way in which their lives had been affected. I could see his visitors were reacting in the same way mine had; shocked, not knowing what to say or do, but being there.

Also in the ward was a young man called Jeff who had also fractured his spine playing sport. Fortunately he'd not injured his spinal cord. Charlene, a nurse with a bright, bubbly personality kept us all amused. She often talked about the men in her life as 'not the full quid' or 'a sausage short of a barbecue.' At other times of people being like, 'pork chops in a synagogue.' She really brightened my day. We all talked to each other, though many of my messages were sent via nurses or visitors.

Ossie had a spinal fusion and after several weeks was allowed to sit out of bed. He had lots of problems with dizziness that continued to plague him for months. Rick, on the other hand, was very reluctant to get out of bed the first time, but on doing so sat up for an hour. Though we are all quadriplegics, we are all different. Gradually Rick, Ossie and Jeff were moved to another part of the ward as their condition improved and new admissions arrived. But being on the ventilator with higher dependency needs, I remained where I was. Though I understood and accepted this, I would have liked to have moved with them.

Four

Journey's End

....

'One door closes another opens.'
Alexander Graham Bell

I wanted to learn more about spinal injuries because even though I am a nurse, there were gaps in my knowledge. Most of the staff, doctors, physiotherapists and nurses recognised that I was well qualified, that I already had a lot of knowledge. They were more than happy to answer my questions. One nurse took the opportunity to teach me on a person-to-person basis. This I appreciated, but unfortunately her teaching was aimed at the lowest common denominator with no recognition for my prior knowledge. One day after giving me a talk on skin care she asked for feedback.

'Well it is all very basic,' I replied candidly and was about to add, 'but good to have it reinforced.'

'I know it's basic,' she snapped and turned on her heel.

What did you expect me to say? I thought as I watched her retreating. *I started nursing when you were still in nappies.*

Following that incident, she started working in another part of the ward. Neither of us felt particularly comfortable with each other. I decided that it was a personality clash as she was well regarded by other patients and staff. I would have liked to have talked it over with her, but as she continued to clearly avoid me I decided that it was her problem and stopped worrying about it.

David looked increasingly tired and haggard. He'd spend all day at work and then came to see me every evening. At weekends he was working on the house or visiting me. I tried to persuade him to have time for himself, but he felt that I needed him and refused. Eventually Helen and I persuaded him to visit friends in New Zealand for two weeks. It was a good break for him. I was glad he went even though I missed him dreadfully and wished that we could have gone together. I also felt jealous that he was able to go and not me.

When I had been in hospital four months, I felt well physically other than the postural problems when I got out of bed. My hearing had improved and I was gradually learning to speak for longer periods with the cuff down. The oedema was starting to disappear and my body felt less bloated. My appetite remained small, but I started to enjoy food more, especially food brought by David or friends.

However, psychologically I was feeling increasingly overwhelmed by all the major decisions we were making about the future, about where to live and about work (both David's and mine). This was exacerbated by the lack of control, plus questions about how we would cope and all this overlaid by feelings of guilt and uselessness. I found it increasingly hard to control my stress levels despite sharing concerns with friends and continuing to practise relaxation.

I then started to experience panic attacks which were very frightening and beyond my control. During these attacks I felt my chest tightening, and I could not breathe. My mind just went into a state of pure panic, I wanted to scream for help. If Maureen or Virginia were on duty, I could sometimes talk it out with them, and other nurses such as Meg I could ask to stay with me until the feelings subsided. But often I had to ask the nurses to hand-ventilate me to relieve the respiratory distress.

Realising I needed help, Maureen suggested I see a psychologist to which I readily agreed. I felt that I was coping with my grief and knew that it was normal to grieve for up to twelve months following a major loss in one's life, but I needed help dealing with the current situation. I met Judie and felt comfortable with her straight away. We found a room where we could talk privately and I told her about some of my concerns. Some things such as my worry about David I initially found too painful to talk about.

We met weekly at first and as I worked through things these sessions were decreased to monthly. She had a few sessions alone with David when he returned from New Zealand, and then we had several sessions together.

Judie used a rational approach to help me look at my concerns. I would make a statement about how I was feeling, for example, 'I feel useless,' and counteract this with a rational statement such as, 'I can use my brain.' I found this a useful technique to shrink my worries and gradually the panic attacks subsided. Though I still had some very down moments, I felt in control.

Judie also taught me a self-hypnosis technique which I found a useful way of letting go of worries and relaxing. Once I had learnt this technique after several sessions, the images were always similar. After going into a hypnotic state, I would come to an oasis in a desert surrounded by palm trees. Sometimes I would arrive in my wheelchair, but I would always get up and walk through a gap in the trees. Inside the oasis the trees changed, often they were beech trees or gum trees and I would look up through their leaves. Sometimes I would float in the warm water of the lake or sit on the sand beside it. Usually there was a gentle breeze blowing. I would then climb into a cocoon lined with plush velvet and relax or float above the oasis feeling warm and secure.

David had some lengthy talks with our friends in New Zealand about our future. They advised him that if he continued to work full time, he would be working to pay people to look after me and have no time to himself. We could both see this and I suggested that I live in an institution and come home at weekends, but David rejected that out of hand. Our marriage was more important than his career. I felt relieved.

After further discussion, we decided to stick to our original plan whereby David would give up work to care for me. I thought about how I would have felt if it was David who was disabled and I knew it was a difficult decision.

We also had to decide where to live, for if we were not working we could no longer afford to live in Sydney. For years we had talked about living in the country, of buying a house mortgage free but enjoy a reasonable quality of life. It would have to be within a couple of hours' drive of a major hospital which restricted where we moved to. We talked a lot about different areas and David started looking around.

After a while Paul came back into hospital following problems with his catheter. Penny said that the arrangements that had been made with home care and the community nurses were not working. There were too many different people coming and she found this very wearing as she was constantly telling people what to do. Paul was able to get twenty-four hours a day nursing care under the third-party insurance scheme, but Penny was refusing to take him home until that was arranged. I wondered why all this had not been sorted out before he left hospital. Professor Chalker suggested that I needed similar care. Though I appreciated his concern, we could not even organise thirty-five hours a week so how could we possibly afford twenty-four hours a day nursing care? Besides, I did not feel I needed such a service.

I would like trained nurses to do my bowel and bladder care and dressings, but the rest of the time I felt David or an attendant (preferably someone with some nursing experience) could see to me.

I asked Paul what he did with his time. He replied that he slept most of the morning and watched television. But Penny said that when he first went home, Paul was reluctant to go out of the house.

What a waste, I thought. *I hope I can find something productive to do.* But I was left wondering how David and I would manage.

I missed my cat and knew that he had pined for me following the accident, but would he know me now? I doubted it after all this time. One of the nurses suggested to David that he bring the cat in one morning and we could sit on the veranda with him. This we did and though I had a familiar smell, there was no longer that instant recognition of which he had before. I felt very sad. We did not bring him in again because like most cats, he hated travelling in cars and peed all over David on the way home, much to David's disgust.

Once I was able to tolerate sitting up in the wheelchair for a few hours, I started rehabilitation with the occupational therapists. This meant a short bus trip down to their department. The rehabilitation sister, Sue, would collect me and hand-ventilate me for the trip there. The bus driver would load and unload the trolley with the ventilator and then return to push me. This was necessary because I was using an ordinary wheelchair and there was no way of attaching the ventilator. Once there the ventilator could be plugged into the electricity and I would be reconnected.

At first, when I went down, I was still wearing the collar but there was a problem as to what to do with me. I couldn't move my arms, so any retraining in this area was pointless. I met Liz, the head occupational therapist, and we started talking about the equipment that I would need such as wheelchairs, commode, bed, weight relieving mattress and cushions. I also looked at some educational videos with one of the other occupational therapists. Once a week we would have a social afternoon and would play Trivial Pursuit with Rick, Ossie and some of the other patients. I always enjoyed these social interactions. It also helped me to talk and to feel comfortable leaving the cuff down for longer periods.

Liz arranged for different equipment to be shown to me so that we could choose the most suitable. One wheelchair demonstration felt particularly strange as Annie (friend and nursing colleague) was with me and I also knew the sales representative from my work. It suddenly struck me that the wheelchair we were looking at was for me and not for a client. I was that disabled person. It was at that point I started to make the transition from being sick to being disabled. Being sick means that it is okay for others to care for you; being disabled means you take responsibility for yourself. At this I found myself grieving all over again for the losses in my life but this time I accepted myself for the way I was and wanted others to do likewise.

'I am not sick, I am physically disabled,' I told them. I also talked more about my physical disability and made jokes about some of the things I could no longer do such as housework. However, I could not talk about my hands; that was still too painful.

My visitors and I were tired of seeing me in hospital gowns. Annie looked at a number of different designs, and we tried two styles of gowns that other friends made for me. The most successful were ones with a yoke, split open down the back and made in a stretch fabric. I had one gown in a bright yellow which one of the nurses really disliked. I teased her initially by deliberately wearing it whenever she was on duty. One of the doctors also fond this amusing, suggesting we ascertain the nurse's birthday and all wear yellow on that day. I enjoyed joking with the staff and found that being able to have a good laugh relieved the seriousness of my situation. For example, when Virginia was explaining to a student how to work my electric bed, she said, 'Take care or Hilary will end up being launched.'

'Then she'll do her space shuttle impersonation,' said Tony Lloyd, one of the dressers. I had images of myself flying off into outer space. What fun!

When Tony realised that I was a nurse he used medical terms to describe what he was doing such as 'lowering the cranium of the bed.' One of the other dressers who was also going grey suggested that we share a bottle of 'Grecian 2000'. I enjoyed these little jokes. After all, life should never be taken too seriously.

The support of friends and family remained very important,

and I always looked forward to visits and letters from them. My sister and another friend sent taped messages, and it was good to hear their voices. I tried taping a message to Gill, but I was so emotional and uptight that it was a miserable failure. Gill sent me a cardigan which she had started knitting on her visit to Australia. She said that she'd not completed it earlier because she could not believe that I would live.

I felt surprised because having survived the accident I never doubted my continued existence. I wondered how many others shared her feelings. However, I knew that this sort of preparatory grief is not uncommon when someone has a serious accident or illness. It allows those people who are close to the victim to prepare for the worst.

When I did not go to therapy I often sat on the veranda or weather permitting, outside under a tree. Initially I felt very nervous about being on my own even though the nurses could hear my alarms from the ward and would check on me regularly. Often, I would wait until I had a visitor before going outside. But after a while I ceased worrying and was quite content to be left on my own. I had to be careful of sunburn because I could not feel the sun on my skin, nor could I move into the shade. Several times I burnt my legs giving them different bands of colour.

'You'll end up looking like a striped bandicoot if you keep burning yourself like that,' Virginia remarked.

Picnics became a regular feature of the weekends and at other times when friends had days off. One pair of friends,

Amy and Rolland, would take me for a walk through the hospital grounds and down to the golf course. Amy would hand-ventilate me and Rolland would push the chair. Apart from these trips I was restricted to short journeys within the hospital grounds with the ventilator placed on a little green trolley. The other patients attending rehabilitation were able to go out with the physiotherapists and OTs once a month on trips to the shopping centre, the cinema and to the Royal National Park. How I longed to go with them, especially the last trip, because it would have been wonderful to be in the bush again. I could not go out with friends and many times David went to different functions without me. I was restricted to the end of an extension cord and became increasingly miserable and frustrated.

After the collar had been off for a week, an X-ray showed that the fracture had slipped. Denis and Meg put the collar back on, and I had to wear it for a few more weeks until the fracture stabilised. During this period Dr Angelis spoke to David and me asking if there was anything we wished to know. She also asked me if was willing to have a phrenic nerve test with a view to having a nerve stimulator implanted. The phrenic nerve passes from the neck into the chest and stimulates the diaphragm, the main muscle of respiration. Due to the damage to my spinal cord, these messages were not getting through to my respiratory muscles which was why I could not breathe without the help of a ventilator. In America and Sweden, they had been implanting phrenic nerve stimulators for a number of years and two such operations had been done in South Australia.

First the phrenic nerve had to be tested to make sure it was working and I agreed for this to be done. Colin and one of the sisters from Intensive Care collected me one morning and took me down to the neurophysiology department. There I met Dr Simpson and Dr MacDonald. In a small room, they had a bank of machines with lots of knobs and dials. Conductor pads were placed on my chest andCed electric charge was administered to stimulate the nerve. I could feel it like the sort of static electricity one receives when touching a car door sometimes. When the charge was increased, I could feel and see my arm jumping and see my chest move. The tests were positive, the stimulated nerves were working.

David wrote to Carol (our social worker friend) at Stoke Manderville Hospital, a large Spinal Injury unit in England. He asked her to find out any information that was available on phrenic nerve implants and she sent us several articles. Lorrain, Dr Angelis and one of the registrars with the rehabilitation team also looked for articles and we exchanged notes. Dr Angelis started gathering information so that she could put in a submission to the board for funding.

From my reading, it appeared that phrenic nerve implant operations had been done for some years. The operation involved implanting two cathodes over the phrenic nerves and feeding two leads with receivers at the end into the chest cavity. Outside the body is a transmitter which sends a message via the phrenic nerves to the diaphragm and the person breathes. The nerves are either stimulated simultaneously or alternately but there seem to be arguments for and against both methods. There were also two types of transmitters; one a small unit which worked on penlight batteries which needed to be changed every day and the other a larger unit with a rechargeable battery plus more flexibility in the controls.

Weaning someone off the ventilator and onto the stimulator had to happen very slowly starting with a few minutes an hour and gradually increasing it until the person was able to tolerate twenty-four hours a day. This had to be done so that the muscle does not become fatigued or the nerve damaged. It can take up to a year to be weaned off the ventilator, and some people continue to use the ventilator at night. Apart from the usual anaesthetic risks and infection, the only complication seemed to be that some people developed spontaneous breathing. This would interfere with the transmitted signal and sometimes have to go back on the ventilator. But one survey showed that all recipients had an improved quality of life.

How wonderful not to be on the ventilator, I thought. I still hated the idea of being kept alive on a machine, and though the stimulator was still an artificial means of respiration, it was somehow more acceptable because it used parts of the real body. Once the first test showed that the nerve was working, I went for a second, more definitive test. This involved swallowing a nasogastric tube to give more accurate measures of how the diaphragm was working. I also met Dr Fletcher, the thoracic surgeon who had agreed to do the operation. During this period, I had a couple of dramas with the tracheostomy. Once when there was a student in the ward, my tubing came adrift. She came over promptly and turned off the alarm but did not realise that she needed to reconnect me. I had no breath left to talk, but I tried to mouth what needed to be done. She continued to turn off the alarm which kept going off but simply stared at me.

Cripes, I thought, *are you going to sit and watch me die?*

'Do you want me to get the sister?' asked my visitor who was thoroughly alarmed as I became increasingly blue.

I nodded my head vigorously. Fortunately, Meg had heard the alarm going off repeatedly and came in from the next ward to investigate and quickly reconnected me.

The second drama occurred when the tracheostomy tube slipped out altogether. With the cuff down there was only a tape holding the tube in place and the tape was loose. There was another student nurse, but this time she notified Meg immediately. She called out to Geoff who immediately slipped the tube back into place. Fortunately, by this stage, I had learnt to hold my breath for several minutes.

I was now very keen to do something useful with my life. If only I could! There were so many things I longed to do. Lea, another friend and colleague of mine, was working on a project for the Department of Health, and she asked me to read and make comments on some of the proposals. It felt really good doing this. The collar had now been removed and I was able to move my neck. Initially it was stiff and became quite sore, but this improved with time. I started typing and painting exercises with Liz in rehabilitation. I also learnt to turn pages of books and sign my name albeit badly. Liz also lent me a page-turner, a machine which turns pages of books and magazines. I had always been an avid reader and it was a real pleasure to be able to read again without relying on others to turn pages for me. I borrowed books on spinal injury and asked Professor Chalker a number of questions as I wanted to improve my knowledge.

Liz arranged for me to go to the Australian Quadriplegic Association Centre so that I could play with their computers. As Sue had to escort me and remain with me for the morning, we went in the bus with the little green trolley. Rick and Ossie were going twice a week for two whole days, but then they had no breathing problems and did not need an escort. How I wished I didn't.

Later Rick did a course in desktop publishing with an excellent teacher from one of the TAFE colleges. I went to a few of the lectures which were very interesting and enjoyable. I was already familiar with the word processing functions of David's personal computer, but this was a different model with different programs. I wore a headset which meant that I had to look at the screen and blow down a tube to click over the commands. This involved a lot of head turning and was frustratingly slow. Liz arranged for a demonstration of a voice-operated computer with an environmental control. It was easy to use and switched quickly from one command to another, but it was very expensive.

People at work had started raising money for me, but so far this was only a small amount. I thought about what I could do and decided to write a recipe book. I asked David if he would bring in his computer so I could use it. Liz arranged to have a stand made for my keyboard so that I could type using a mouth stick which was much quicker than the headset. Unfortunately after I had written a few letters, the disc drive stopped working, and took weeks to get repaired. More frustration.

I started to attend patient education talks on the ward. These were one to two-hour sessions on a variety of topics such as skin care, sexuality and community services. Though much of this information was familiar to me because of my nursing background, I was still interested in what people had to say. I offered to give a talk on communication skills and assertiveness to the other patients. The Occupational Therapy Department now had their own computer and I used this to design overheads and wrote a hand-out. David printed the overheads onto plastic sheets at work. I was anxious about giving a talk. Could I still do it? Would my voice fade? How would the other patients respond to me? Meg helped by putting on the overheads which I used to illustrate my talk. It was a fairly quiet group of fellow patients but other than that it went well and they all gave me positive feedback.

The OTs then asked me to give a similar talk for their in-service. To our surprise Liz was asked by the psychologists to justify what I was doing. We were both angry that they had not spoken directly to me, after all I am an adult and capable of making my own decisions. It had never occurred to me that I would be stepping on anyone's toes and I had presumed that the psychologists had more than enough work to do. Judie spoke with me about this later and explained that they were worried about the medico-legal implications and whether I would harm anyone. I assured her that I was appropriately qualified and experienced and aware of the limitations of my skills. She was also concerned as to whether I was ready to talk to others – but surely that was for me to decide. Though I continued to meet and talk with Judie, I felt that our relationship had changed and left wondering whether she regarded me as a person or a patient.

I was now taking much more interest in my fellow patients and wished that I had an electric wheelchair so I could move around freely and talk to them. David had developed a lot of skills, and many relatives told me that they had gained a lot of support and comfort by talking with him. Two young men, both in their teens, had been admitted to the ward; Alfred, a paraplegic and Mike, a quadriplegic. Both had met up with an old school friend who had suggested going for a drive. It had ended with a car crash severely injuring the pair.

How terrible, I thought, *to be injured at the commencement of your adult life.* At least I had had the opportunity to build a career, travel and enjoy the pleasures of so many things.

Though I knew that these young men could also do many things, disability does limit your choices. It was not only their lives that were affected but their family's lives too. David and I spent a lot of time talking to them and their families. Mike's mother was especially angry for what had happened to her son and for all their lost hopes and dreams. She was seeing one of the psychologists and I encouraged her to keep doing so even though she was tempted to stop these sessions. But I could understand. Anger is a normal part of the grieving process and frequently directed towards staff, as her feelings often were.

One of the OTs, Valerie, ran a group for the psychiatric patients and asked whether I would give a talk to them on the issue of loss. I thought very carefully about this; was I ready? I had never talked to a group of people with psychiatric problems before. How could I make what I had to say relevant to them? I asked Amy for her advice. I decided that I could do it and made arrangements with Sue to take me there. Following this they asked me to give another talk which I did on Self Talk. Had I not developed a pressure sore I would have done more.

David finally accepted help from friends and finished painting the house. We put it up for sale and on the day that we put the house on the market, David returned home late at night to find that someone had tried to break in. Being unsuccessful, they had smashed a stained-glass door panel that David had made. We were both very upset by this incident. The house took several months to sell as the market was slow. David worried constantly as to whether we would sell it at a reasonable price and be able to buy something else. No matter how we did the sums, we could not afford to stay in Sydney unless David worked full-time and took out a larger mortgage. He started looking at housing in areas north and south of Sydney. Because of my need for the ventilator, we needed to be within a couple of hours' drive of a major hospital. David would come back from these outings looking increasingly depressed, we could afford to buy something, but it would be very ordinary. Owning our own house meant that we would have security and be better off financially in our reduced financial circumstances.

We had good friends in Adelaide who had suggested that we move there. I had been reluctant because it meant leaving friends behind, but now we decided that David should go to South Australia and look around. This he did and he took a video of various places around Adelaide, looking at the price of land plus the cost of building a home. After much discussion, we decided that when the house was sold, David would go again to look at land in Strathalbyn, a small town fifty kilometres from Adelaide. He also brought back house plans as we decided it would be easier to have a house built rather than alter an existing dwelling. Two plans were suitable, one a mud brick home, but it meant David doing a lot of the work himself as well as caring for me. The other plan was for a project home which we finally settled on after a lot of discussion with Helen and Liz. Neither plan needed much alteration to make the house suitable for my needs.

David became increasingly stressed and lonely. I tried to encourage him to go out but was envious when he did so. I felt that life was passing me by and was increasingly miserable that I could no longer live as I once did. Peter from work came to say goodbye as he was leaving and I wished that I could have gone to his farewell. We both felt very sad as we had worked well together.

Paul came back into hospital for a minor operation. He lent me his wheelchair. For the first and only time in the twelve months I was in hospital, I went on an outing with the therapists. My mother was down again, and she came with us to the races. It was a cold day, so we had to rug up well. I found Paul's chair hard to manoeuvre especially turning to the left. After leaving the racetrack I discovered the chin control unit did not work. I worried it was something that I had done, but fortunately only a loose wire which was soon repaired.

In August the rehabilitation team had its annual picnic, and as I still could not go far, we decided to have it in the grounds of the hospital near the chapel so that we could plug my ventilator into the electricity supply. It was a warm but windy day and we spent most of the afternoon eating and talking. It was good to be with the team again and to catch up on all the gossip. I longed to be able to return to work.

Five

Black Hole

....

*'There is only one way out of this place,
and that is in a box.'*

I had now been in hospital for eight months, and I was physically and psychologically ready to go home, but how could I? I had no equipment, no care organised and nowhere to live. I felt increasingly frustrated. Liz had been prompt in collating a list of all the equipment I needed and sent this to the PADP committee. As the total cost of this equipment was over twenty thousand dollars, which is a large slice out of anyone's budget, the committee applied to the Department of Health for special funding. Even though the funds were not forthcoming, the application was sent on to the board of the amalgamated hospitals.

Liz and I had to write a submission explaining why we had chosen a more costly wheelchair in preference of another cheaper model. Then we had to write a list of essential equipment and why it was required. All this took time and I felt angry that a submission for funding had not been put in earlier. Though concerned about the high cost of the equipment, I also felt frustrated at needlessly tying up a hospital bed. All this was at a considerably greater cost to the taxpayer in the long run than the value of the equipment I was seeking; a ridiculous situation.

I had no alternative but to apply for PADP funding as I was not eligible for compensation nor did we have private savings to cover this amount. Without this equipment I could not live at home with the result that I would be forced to lie in a nursing home bed for the rest of my life. If that was the case, what was the point of resuscitating me in the first place? I had been given no choice over whether I lived or died, but if I could not be offered a reasonable quality of life. Why bother?

Likewise, with the submission for care, we had received no word as to whether my application had been approved even though the submission had been sent over three months earlier. I worried that I would be ready to go home without care being organised.

Where to live was yet another problem, as we had put the house on the market and now had to wait for a buyer. We had decided to move to South Australia and build a house, but this depended on how much we could get for our present house. It was another source of worry and the old house was threatening to become a millstone around David's neck.

A further problem was where to live while the new house was being built. We tossed about various ideas. The social worker suggested we put in an application for Berala, a joint Paraquad / Department of Housing development designed for people with spinal injuries. People are allowed to stay in such houses for twelve months while they sort out their lives. In addition to a number of individual two and three-bedroom houses, there was to be a training centre with bed-sitting rooms. At that stage, Berala in Sydney's west was not completed and way behind schedule. Despite the worry it would not be ready when I was, we put in an application. We were invited to inspect one of the houses which David did. I could not go because I did not have a suitable wheelchair or a battery for the ventilator, one that would last for longer than an hour; a constant source of frustration for me.

I had developed a pressure area on my left heel shortly after I was transferred to the spinal unit and though I was shocked at the size of the black, necrosed area, it did not stop me getting out of bed. Then I developed a second small pressure area in the crease between my buttock and my left thigh. This was more serious because it prevented me from getting up. It was possibly caused by the elastic in my underwear or by the commode chair. I was astounded when one of the nurses announced, 'Oh yes, I noticed a red spot there two days ago'. He'd said nothing nor had he advised me to stay in bed until the red area disappeared. It is all very well to say that I am responsible for my skincare, but because I couldn't see or feel the pressure on my back, I was still reliant on others to tell me if there was a problem. Whatever happened to his duty of care?

The thought of spending a day in bed let alone a month was devastating. I refused to eat that day but realised that this was detrimental to my health and ate properly the next day. I was also worried that I might develop chest problems through lying in bed. I asked Regina if I could get up for two hours per day in order to continue attending rehabilitation. She reluctantly agreed because there was a saying that you could put anything on a pressure area except the patient. However, the pressure sores did improve albeit slowly.

Up until now I had very flaccid paralysis, though I had noted an occasional twitch of a toe or finger, I soon started to have spasms. Spasms are spontaneous muscle contractions that may be brought on by a movement, a touch, or a skin problem. The spasms which I experienced can be divided into three types; those involving the whole body, those involving a limb and clonus (shaking) spasms. None of them are severe, and therefore I take nothing for them unlike some people with a spinal injury who experience severe spasms that can throw them out of their chair.

Following my accident, I had ceased to menstruate which is a normal occurrence following severe trauma. My periods then returned with a vengeance and I had an increase in spasm especially if someone touched me on the stomach or in the pubic region. I also felt hyperreflexia especially when having my bowel care and once I experienced a severe headache. It was as though my brain was trying to push through my skull. If this was what it is like to be seriously hyperreflexic, I would rather not know. Hyperreflexia (also known as dysreflexia) occurs due to complex physiological changes in the body. The blood in the lower part of the body rushes to above the level of the lesion causing a life-threatening rise in blood pressure and severe headaches. This concerned me and I asked Professor Chalker if his registrar could contact my gynaecologist to ask whether I should go back on the pill which I had been taking for endometriosis. But they did not seem to think that was necessary. I accepted their decision and fortunately the next time I menstruated I experienced only a mild headachy feeling, though I continued to have an increase in spasm at these times.

With the onset of menstruation and subsequent periods, I noted that a number of female nurses never mentioned to me that I was menstruating. Did they think that I knew? The only way that I could tell was either by being told or seeing the blood. Some nurses just slid an incontinence sheet under me and seemed reluctant to give me a pad unless I pestered them. This practice disgusted me. Just because I was disabled did not mean that I didn't have the same needs as other women. I was both surprised and puzzled by this attitude. Surely menstruation is not a taboo subject in this day and age?

I was able to tolerate having my tracheostomy cuff down all day and could talk freely at last. However, there were still times when communication was difficult because I relied mostly on speech but unable to give many other visual cues. Though I tried to explain myself clearly, it was sometimes difficult to find the right words. I felt as frustrated with myself as I did with the other person when I could not make myself understood. Though it had not been a particular problem before, I sometimes found speaking with people for whom English is a second language very difficult. One day to my horror and embarrassment I found myself shouting at one of the nurses. At other times I tried too hard. One day I asked one of the dressers, 'Could you do this, could you do that,' when he replied with patient irritation, 'Of course I can, Hilary.' I realised that I was sounding like a kindergarten teacher and to the embarrassment of both of us I burst into tears. Why was good communication so difficult?

Many of the nurses started asking my advice on nursing issues and we often spent time discussing the current problems with nursing. Lack of recognition of the work that nurses do and inadequate remuneration have been and still are chronic problems. It was ten years since I'd worked in a hospital, but was surprised at how little had changed. The division between the different departments and the non-recognition of people less qualified or lower down the pecking order also remain chronic problems. In addition, there was a shortage of nursing staff, and the nurses often worked double shifts or worked with nurses employed through an agency; some of whom did not know the hospital. I often wondered how the nurses coped. There was also continual talk of the hospital closing and the transfer of the spinal unit to a number of different sites which had an unsettling effect on all the staff.

On the positive side, there was a team spirit and many of the nurses had worked in the unit for a number of years. Many of the patients who were admitted to the acute section of the spinal ward were anxious and confused following their trauma. I can only express my admiration for the nurses who treated these people with patience and a sense of humour. My only major criticism of the unit was that there was no discharge planner. This is a person, usually a nurse, who is actively involved in the patient's discharge. They are able to liaise with different departments, tie all the loose ends together and act as a patient advocate. This means that instead of speaking to several people about their discharge, the patient and their relatives need only speak to one person.

I had to make a decision about returning to work because up until now I had been on sick leave and long service leave, but this was now starting to run out. David contacted a friend in the state superannuation board who gave good advice on applying for an invalid pension. I then contacted the personnel officer at work who started the difficult process of getting the pension granted to me.

Up until this time I'd played with various ideas as to how I could return to work without being a drain on resources. Now I had to think seriously about what I could do. Obviously, I could not return to work in a practical sense as a nurse, but I hoped to continue teaching stress management courses. Had we been staying in Sydney I would have seriously considered returning to work in an administrative capacity, but now I planned and dreamed about what I could do in Strathalbyn. David and I talked a lot about what we could do there.

In November we sold the house and David had the major task of packing our belongings, most of which had to go into storage. Again I felt useless and wished that we could be doing this together. I also felt sad that I would never see my home again and used the self-hypnosis technique to visit the various rooms in the house and say goodbye. David made another trip to South Australia, bought a block of land in Strathalbyn and talked to the builder about getting a house built. He took a video of the land and surrounding area so that I could see where our future home was to be.

Finally, after nine and a half months, my electric wheelchair arrived and I had to learn to drive it. This was difficult because I could not use my hands. I drove the chair with a chin control. Initially I tended to slip off the control and steer into walls and doorways. Once when returning from rehabilitation, the bus driver was trying to help me reverse back into the space beside my bed when we crashed into another patient's bed. Though his visiting father got a shock, the patient was quite unconcerned and kept eating his dinner. Fortunately, his fracture was stable, so no damage was done.

I still could not go far as we did not have a lead to connect the ventilator to the battery. We had to wait a few weeks for the next shipment to arrive before David could go to the supplier and pick it up.

Nothing ever seemed to happen smoothly. In the meantime, we made arrangements for me to get my hair cut at the local shopping centre and contacted the hairdresser about plugging in the ventilator whilst I was there. A few months previously I had my hair cut all the same length by a hairdresser who visited the hospital. She spent five minutes chopping my hair, but I was not happy with the result. There was no problem about getting me to the hairdressers as David had purchased a van and we had a hoist fitted with financial assistance from the Commonwealth Rehabilitation Service. This meant that I could be lifted into the back of the van in my wheelchair which was then held in place by clamps on the floor.

However, I was not to get to the hairdresser because I took a risk by sitting up most of the day and my pressure area deteriorated markedly. In the morning, I'd give a talk to the psychiatric patients and in the afternoon, I'd attend rehabilitation. That evening Helen and I wove a very uncertain path down to the chapel where we had a picnic. I'd taken this risk based on the belief that the upper pressure area was healing and was therefore astounded when the nurse again said, 'Oh yes, I noticed that it was looking worse two days ago.'

He had said nothing to me nor to the other staff, and I could not understand it. This time I was really angry and said so. It now meant that I had to stay in bed and I wondered how I would pass the time. I read and listened to music and audio tapes. When the computer was finally fixed, I started writing this book and a recipe book; I also wrote letters. The time still passed very slowly and I had too much time to think. I felt very depressed.

Geoff suggested that I lie on my right side as much as possible to relieve the pressure on the sore. But I found this difficult because it put a strain on my neck muscles which sometimes became intolerably painful in two hours or less. I needed to rest on my back after being on my side. Had the staff been able to turn my hips and left my shoulders fairly flat this would not have been such a problem. However, most staff seemed unable to grasp this concept and would turn my whole body. Sometimes I was so far over, almost on my front, that it restricted my breathing. Geoff also insisted that I lie only on my right side rather than from side to side which I preferred. I would have still been off the sore. I tried to argue against only lying on my right side rather than from side to side. In the end, I reluctantly agreed to comply.

One day my left shoulder became unbearably sore from the strain put upon it through lying on my right side. I was getting such strong spasm in the region of the left shoulder blade that I felt like I was being kicked in the back by a mule. So I insisted on being turned on my left side too. After a few days, the pain and spasm decreased, but I continue to have problems with my left shoulder. Liz had noted that my left shoulder was subluxed several weeks before. This happens when the head of the humerus drops out of the shoulder joint. This is fairly common when someone has a paralysed arm and care has to be taken to support the arm properly, such as never letting it hang over the side of the bed or chair.

I thought about why the left arm was affected but not the right one and I decided that because my ventilator was on the right side of the bed everyone tended to turn me that way. In addition, they often unconsciously pulled on the left shoulder, or the arm fell down over the side of the bed. Being aware of this and asking that these practices be avoided plus insisting that I turn to the left as well as the right helped improve this situation.

The other problem with only lying on one side was that I developed another wax blockage in my left ear which plugged and unplugged depending upon what position I was in. I also developed a skin rash on my face which was terribly itchy and distressing as I had always had clear skin. I noted that it was worse if I was upset or if I had a blocked catheter, and put this rash down to the stress and frustration I was feeling. I believed that it would improve when I went home. The doctor ordered a hydrocortisone cream which relieved the itch, but the rash continued to come and go.

When the ward was busy, it was difficult to get my hair washed because this procedure involved being lifted up off the bed by two dressers and having my hair washed by two nurses. Several times my scalp became very scaly and itchy. I always looked forward to Helen's visits as among other things, she always gave my hair a good brush.

Jeff had gone home some months before, but he continued to visit me when he attended outpatient clinics. Then Rick and Ossie went home, and though I had only seen them once or twice a week at rehabilitation, I experienced an overwhelming sense of loss and loneliness. 'Everyone goes home except me,' I complained bitterly to Helen.

However, I continued to be visited by other patients and their relatives especially Alfred and Mike and their families. I appreciated this because I knew that many of the patients did not like visiting the acute end of the ward because of the bad memories associated with their early post-trauma days.

In December the final settlement on the house took place and David had to find somewhere for him and the cat to live. We had hoped that Berala would be completed so that David would not have to move twice but this was not to be. The cat went to live with a friend but traumatised by the move he started peeing on her walls. Eventually, we put him in a cattery. David put some of our furniture in storage, left other things with a friend and moved in to share a house with some young people from work.

Though this was satisfactory as far as their relationships were concerned, David felt very unsettled because he was living out of suitcases. As he was so miserable, I hoped that Berala would be completed soon, but we kept getting conflicting dates and started to live from week to week.

At this stage I still had heard nothing about care, and worried I would be ready to leave hospital before it was approved. I asked the social worker and friends to find out what was happening through their various contacts. It appeared that the submission was waiting for approval by the Minister of

Community Services and Health. We decided to write to him and pointed out that it cost more to keep me in hospital than it did to provide me with care.

Just before Christmas, I asked Professor Chalker if I could attend the rehabilitation team's staff Christmas lunch, an annual event. This was extremely important to me because it would be the last such lunch that I would have with my staff as we would be living in South Australia the following year. Also, I wanted to see how comfortable I felt with the staff even though I'd seen most of them while in hospital. Though I accepted that it was necessary to ask Professor Chalker, I did feel a certain resentment at being unable to suit myself. He, of course, gave permission and the two drivers from work came to pick me up in the bus.

What gentle caring men they both were. I had often wondered what it was like to be lifted by the hoist into a bus when sitting in a wheelchair but I felt confident and secure with those two. As is their wont, they drove slowly and carefully, avoiding the many potholes. Ron tied a harness around my shoulders because I kept falling to one side especially when we went around corners. I felt quite happy to arrive at work where we picked up the rest of the staff and drove on to a restaurant. All the staff who knew me previously kissed me on the cheek and the new staff introduced themselves. It was like returning to a family. We had a good lunch and I enjoyed talking with the team. All too soon it was over, and I had to return.

The ward had a pre-Christmas party for patients and their

relatives and Regina arranged for me to have my bed wheeled up to the other end of the ward. However, much to David's annoyance I was a real wet blanket. I was feeling down because I did not want to be in hospital. I wanted more than anything to be free to move around and talk to people, not stuck in bed. Ossie was back in hospital because he had developed a pressure area and I asked that my bed be pushed closer to his so I could talk with him, but even this was awkward.

Having spent my birthday, David's birthday and our wedding anniversary in hospital, the thought of spending Christmas in hospital was unbearable. I again asked Professor Chalker if David and I could go to a hotel for the Christmas period. It would be a final splurge before living in reduced financial circumstances, and David booked into the Regent Hotel. Noel from Paraquad gave me his phone number and though we did not need to contact him, it was reassuring to know that we could.

On Christmas Eve, David and Helen loaded me into the van. Equipped with a hoist, suction equipment and continence aids, we took off for the city. Gone were the carefree days when we could jump into the car and go wherever we wished. The van had stiff suspension and I bounced and flopped around in the back. I clearly needed some sort of harness to stop me falling sideways in the chair. We arrived at the hotel and I managed to steer myself across the lobby without demolishing anyone or anything. We had a delightful lunch but then Helen left us and David and I retired to our room.

We had lovely views of Circular Quay and the harbour and I was content to be with David, to sit and look at the view. How my world had shrunk. Shortly after we established ourselves in the room a large platter of fruit and cheese plus a bottle of wine arrived, compliments of David's colleagues at work. Lee called in later that afternoon and helped us eat some of it. It was so good to be out of hospital.

When David went to put me into bed that night we found that the feet of the hoist would not fit under the bed because it had a solid base; something we'd not anticipated. David managed to roll me onto the bed, and it was lovely to lie beside him, to know he was there. I was also pleased that David still found me sexually attractive because this was something I had wondered about during those long ten months in hospital. Sometimes I wondered whether he had been tempted to find a girlfriend, not that he would have had time between working full-time and visiting me.

On Christmas Day the community nurse called and attended to my dressings. Following a breakfast of fresh rolls and percolated coffee, a friend came and helped David to dress me. Getting out of bed was a problem as we could not use the hoist. I suggested that they put pillows on the floor and roll me out of bed on to them and then use the hoist. This they did, and it worked quite well though I noted that both of them were sweating because of the exertion. After our friend left, we went downstairs and David loaded me into the van and we set off for Christmas lunch at another friend's place.

The Day I Fell off My Bicycle

As the entrance to their house was up a steep flight of stairs, we had borrowed a manual chair from the hospital. When we arrived, they lifted me into this chair and our friend took control of the ventilator. As they started taking me backwards up the stairs, the wheels caught on the steps as the tyres were flat. David pushed the chair forward to release the wheels, but unfortunately, the friends at the front of the chair let it drop down. I slithered out of the chair and ended up in a crumpled heap at the bottom of the steps. I did not fall far, nor did I hurt myself or the ventilator as a friend was still holding it. When I looked at the shocked faces around me, I burst out laughing. Once my friends had recovered from their shock, they joined me. We then decided to carry the chair up the steps and then they would carry me. Following a delicious lunch with good company, we ventured down the steps without mishap this time then returned to the hotel. It had been a great Christmas.

When we passed through the hotel foyer, we crossed paths with a group of Japanese tourists who were going out of the main door. I stopped to let them pass, and they stopped to let me pass. As my driving was still haphazard, I thought it safer to let them go first. To my amusement, they all bowed very low as they passed me.

The following day I persuaded David to ask for help to transfer me from the bed to the chair, and in due course the security guard arrived. He was about six foot six and equally broad across the shoulders; he lifted me as though I was a feather. It was very hot and humid. I would have liked to have gone to Circular Quay but as I could not control my body temperature and tended to take on the surrounding air temperature, I reluctantly agreed to return to hospital. I did however, with Regina's permission, visit the other patients before returning to bed.

In the period following Christmas I hit rock bottom. Though most of my equipment had arrived, there was still no word as to when Berala would be completed, no word about attendant care and no improvement in my pressure area. On my return, Regina had inspected the area and said that my Christmas trip had not affected it adversely. However, one of the nurses who had not seen the problem for a month stated that it looked exactly the same as when she had last seen it earlier. If that was the case, it meant I'd spent a whole month in bed for nothing.

I was also very angry that I was still in hospital and this time did not care who knew. I was fed up with thinking of others, of trying to be cheerful and wanted to wallow in my angry despair. I was fed up in being in a section with a lot of acutely ill people. I took no interest in them but continued talking with the patients who visited me from the other part of the ward. Often, I shut the world out by closing my eyes and listening to the radio. Things that I'd tolerated previously now started to irritate me intensely. Asking for things to be done became an anathema. Because the ward was busy I often went for days without having my hair brushed, and my toenails became long and ingrown. I forgot to take my tablets if they were left on the locker.

One of the nurses, Rudolph, was very unsettled. Initially I had listened sympathetically to his complaints as had the other staff, but his continual carping criticism of others, the hospital and the New South Wales health system was too much. Often, I pretended that I was asleep so that I did not have to talk with him and was relieved when he resigned even though I wished him well.

At the time I was reading Stephen Hawkins' book, *A Brief History of Time*. I wished that like his imaginary astronaut, I could be sucked into a black hole and turned into nothing much. I felt as though I was looking into a deep dark hole.

'There is only one way out of this place and that is in a box,' I said to David.

I thought of ways in which I could end my life. The endless day after day in hospital had become unbearable. In recent years I had worried about developing cancer. But now I took a perverse delight in imagining a cancer-like black spider growing in my womb and spreading its hairy legs into the other organs of my body. Had I been able to get up in my chair I would have found some way to take my own life. I thought constantly as to how I could do this. Because I was so angry, I did not share my thoughts with anyone. I just wanted it all to end. Was there no way out?

Some people may wonder why I did not talk to Judie about how I was feeling but following the incident about the talk to the therapists, that sense of trust had gone. Reprieve came in the middle of January when Berala was finally ready, and David was able to move into a two bedroom house.

'What do you think the street is called?' David asked when he visited one night.

'Don't know,' I said.

'Dire Straits,' he replied with a grin.

I burst out laughing as did friends when told. Apparently, Paraquad had obtained permission to auction the names of the streets at a charity function. Then the rock band *Dire Straits* in Sydney at the time had bought the street name. Though all this caused us considerable amusement, we wondered how other residents felt about it.

David was very happy to move into more permanent accommodation and unpack our things. He also collected the cat who spent the first two weeks hiding in the cupboard and after that a week hiding under the bed, but eventually settled down.

At the same time, my application for attendant care was approved. Carmon from Paraquad came to see me about recruiting attendants. We decided to place advertisements in the local papers and got a very good response. As I was still in hospital, I asked Carmon to be the first contact and to select people for interview. She chose four people whom she brought to the hospital for me to meet. Three were satisfactory, and we decided to employ them.

I believe that it is very important for the person with

a disability to be able to choose his or her own attendants because compatibility is a very important factor in their relationship. The person doing the selection needs to have clear ideas as to what's expected of the attendants and vice versa. For example, I chose people who had previous experience of caring for others and who could drive. In addition to attending to my personal care, I asked my attendants to help with washing and housework. We also discussed the hours which I wanted them to work so that we all had a clear understanding of what the job entailed.

In addition to personal care attendants, a referral was made to a Community Nursing Service and to Home Care. Shaun from Home Care came to meet me in the hospital to discuss what I would like help with. He asked how I felt about having a man assisting with my personal care at home and I reassured him this was not a problem. Lydia, a community nurse and clinical nurse specialist in spinal injuries also came to see me about my nursing care. We agreed that the nurses would come three days a week to attend to my bowel care and to shower me, and a further two other days to attend to my dressings.

Lydia discussed my nursing needs with the ward staff and made arrangements for two of the nurses working in the Berala area to come to the hospital to meet me. They also observed how to suction me, practised using my hoist and showered me a few times. Once when they showered me I promptly blacked out, possibly because I'd been lying fairly flat before getting out of bed. Meg was with us and advised the nurses to tilt the back of the chair back and I recovered very quickly. It became a standard joke between Meg and myself that I only did dramatic things when she was present.

In addition to this, I had to arrange for someone to change my tracheostomy tube every four to six weeks. Helen contacted the surgical registrar at the hospital where the rehabilitation service was based and he agreed to do this. Otherwise it would have meant a long trip back into the hospital every time the tube needed changing. I would have preferred to have contacted the doctor myself when I left hospital, but the staff insisted that the arrangements be made before I left. Again I felt resentment at not having control over my life.

The community nurses had a rule that they would not change a suprapubic catheter which had been in place less than twelve months. Therefore, I asked Annie if she would do this for me and made arrangements for her to see one such catheter change. I also asked the nurses to instruct my attendants about my personal care and in particular how to suction me. Unfortunately, there was no organised program for training attendants and the nurses had to combine this with their other duties.

Though I made a time with the nurses and asked them to show my attendants the two most essential aspects of my care, namely how to suction me and hand-ventilate, the nurses only gave them a brief demonstration. It would have been preferable if my attendants could have done these things under their supervision, but the nurses seemed unwilling to let my attendants practise while I was in hospital. I found this frustrating and continued to feel apprehensive about this aspect of my care. I told David we would have to train my attendants ourselves at home.

Now that I finally had somewhere to live and people to care for me, I could organise a date for my discharge. I asked Professor Chalker if I could leave hospital in a month and I hoped that this would give the staff sufficient time to organise the aids necessary for my ongoing care. Though I jokingly told staff that I was planning an escape, I did feel that I would at last be free to live my own life.

When one of the other patient's relatives asked me if I was going home for a trial period, I looked at her in horror. Other patients did go home for weekends and visits prior to their discharge from hospital to ensure that everything was as it should be. However, neither Paul nor myself could leave the hospital grounds until we had a suitable chair with a ventilator battery, lead and connection. Neither of us had gone home prior to our discharge. I had been in hospital nearly twelve months and had no intention of returning except for the phrenic nerve implant. David had shown at Christmas that he could look after me and I felt confident in organising my carers. Though I still had the pressure area, this was no reason for remaining in hospital. In fact, I had lost confidence in the hospital staff's ability to heal the sore and thought I would be better off at home. At least I would eat properly which I was not doing - having come to hate hospital food.

Discharging anyone from hospital is often complex especially where there are a large number of factors to be considered as in my case. These factors included equipment, care, organising who would change my tracheostomy tube and urinary catheter and a supply of aids, such as suction catheters for three months, arrangements for future supplies, medications and discharge letters. That is why good discharge planning is so important. Good coordination between departments is essential but often falls down because staff are trying to organise these things on top of other duties. Even though I had been in hospital twelve months and had given a month's notice of my intention to leave, I still left without all this sorted out.

ProfessorChalker advised me that the first submission for the phrenic nerve stimulator had been rejected because it was "new" technology. He and Dr Angelis would put together another submission with more information and support from their colleagues. Professor Chalker seemed confident of their success and advised me that he would contact me when everything was arranged. I was happy to leave it in their hands but one of the nurses said, 'Don't hold your breath waiting.' Under the circumstances I found that hilarious.

As this was to be the first such operation in New South Wales, all the staff were very interested as to what was involved. When I told Rita, one of the nurses, she said, much to my amusement, that I would be able to talk to the truckies via the transmitter. I returned once more to the neurophysiology department for a final check that the nerves were still working and there was no change since the last tests.

Because it was twelve months since I had become a quadriplegic, I went for urodynamic studies to check that my bladder was functioning satisfactorily. This meant that I had to stop taking the tablets for my bladder for a few days but I felt continuously nauseated.

There was now a last-minute flurry of activity. Should I have an oxygen cylinder and mask at home? Arrangements were made for me to have an alarm system installed and there was a concern that I might die at home. This irritated me. I felt that it was an intrusion on my personal wishes because I'd long ago accepted the possibility of death and no longer worried about it. I felt that it would have been more appropriate to have trained my attendants how to suction me correctly because this was an everyday essential requirement that needed to be done as necessary.

The nurses had to prepare a list of the consumables, such as humidifiers for the ventilator, which I would need for the next three months. This was in addition to their normal ward duties, and I worried whether everything would be ready in time. However, Charlene was working in the acute part of the ward and it was impossible to feel miserable while she was there. I also joked with the other nurses, and Meg peeled me a grape when feeding me lunch one day. Personally I preferred them with the skin on.

Finally the day arrived. After delays waiting for medications and letters and humidifiers to arrive, I said goodbye to the nurses who'd cared for me all those long months. I felt a little sad but thought that I would see them soon when I returned for the operation for the phrenic nerve stimulator. Twelve months and two weeks after the day I fell off my bike I went to my new home.

Six

In Dire Straits

....

*'Living is something you do now or never
– which do you do?'*
Piet Hein

The trip home was uneventful. Liz had given me a harness which went around my shoulders and the chair and this greatly improved my problem of flopping. When we arrived at the house, a large group of children who lived in the street gathered to watch me being unloaded and to ask numerous questions. I felt that I was on show, and wished that I could have given them a royal wave. Sitting on the front step was a basket of fruit and flowers from the rehabilitation team. They were going to include a message, 'Free, Hallelujah, free at last,' but changed their minds.

I was home and it was wonderful to see all our familiar things; furniture, paintings and pottery. I had never realised how much they meant to me. David prepared dinner, and it felt strange to watch him doing all the work because previously we had shared it. I felt so useless. It was good to have dinner together and to be able to talk privately. I slept well that night.

The following morning two of the community nurses arrived to attend to my personal care. They also asked a number of questions so that they could develop a plan for my care. As I still had the pressure sore on my thigh, I decided to stay in bed and only get up when I wanted to go somewhere or do something.

On Saturday we asked Carmon and my attendants, Daniella, Trish and Anomi to come around. This was so that we could show them where things were kept, how my various pieces of equipment worked and ensure that they could suction me correctly. Unfortunately, Daniella could not come because her sister had died and she had flown to Perth for the funeral and to spend time with the family.

Trish was the person with most experience, having worked in nursing homes and the Multiple Sclerosis centre. She had also cared for people with spinal injuries at home. She was efficient and a good organiser. Initially this caused a little friction between us because I wanted to organise my own life. Anomi also had experience working in nursing homes. I am sure she will forgive me for saying that she was not the most practical person and definitely not mechanically minded. However, she was a very funny lady and we enjoyed many good laughs together. Daniella was the least experienced, but very warm and caring and willing to learn. I had some reservations about employing her because she thought that I would get better. Having accepted the reality of my situation, I now felt uncomfortable with people who had unrealistic expectations about my recovery.

Once I'd established that I knew what I wanted and needed, we got on well. Daniella was a good cook and when she cooked for her family, she'd bring a meal for David and me. Following a short period of adjustment, we soon came to trust each other. Having good attendants was essential because David was working two days a week and often went out on his days off. If a life-threatening situation occurred, they had to know what to do.

In the evening Shaun from Home Care helped put me back to bed. He was a very likeable young man who was a qualified psychiatric nurse and had experience in caring for people with spinal injuries. In addition, his wife was also a quadriplegic and had a great depth of understanding as to what it meant to be disabled. Because he was so capable, David often felt inadequate even though he really liked Shaun. When I rang my sister, Gill, I told her that I had a nice young man to help me into bed and she expressed her jealousy. Shaun looked embarrassed when I laughingly repeated it to him. We did not know each other well enough yet.

On the following Monday Lydia arrived with two nurses and Carmon arrived with Anomi and Trish all to see how to shower me. Carmon retired discretely to talk with David. It was all a bit of a circus as people fell over each other trying to do things. It was crowded in the bedroom which was not designed for so many plus a commode and hoist. I found the whole situation rather funny.

After that things settled down. The nurses came five days a week, usually on their own unless they were instructing someone new or on Fridays when David was home. I appreciated this as I preferred that David not be involved with my bowel care, so the personal and sexual side of our relationship was not affected. Having once worked with the same nursing service, I got on well with all the nurses and did not mind the sometimes frequent and unavoidable change of staff. Everyone who came received prior instruction on how to care for my special needs and I appreciated not having to tell people how to do things.

Having helpers also meant that David could do a little part-time work which helped supplement the cost of my care. Our financial situation was vastly different to what it was before my accident when we were both working. We wondered how we would survive. It also meant that David could have a day to himself to do the things he wanted and to relax, but usually he went shopping.

For David it was a much bigger period of adjustment. While in hospital I'd become used to a daily routine and to having a number of different people caring for me. Though Lorrain had instructed him how to suction me and he'd watched the nurses do my dressings, this was a new situation. There were so many things to think about, and he worried whether he was caring for me properly. If only he had received more instruction whilst I was still in hospital. I tried to help as much as possible by asking appropriately for things to be done and establishing a routine, but the burden of responsibility still weighed heavily on him. Sometimes I smiled to myself wryly because prior to my accident I had enjoyed doing things at the spur of the moment. Sadly, those days were gone forever. At times David became much hassled and frustrated because he did not have enough time to do all the things he wanted. Sometimes I could be philosophical about this and think that things would get better when we were more established, but at other times I would get angry too.

'I'm not a bloody nuisance,' I would shout at him. 'Do you really think I want to be like this? Do you know what it's like?'

If only I could have done a little more for myself, it would have relieved the pressure on both of us. David had to adjust also to having strange people in the house. Sometimes becoming frustrated when people put things back in the wrong place and he could not find them. As I had never lived in the house before I could not tell people where things went either. I was not much help. With so many people coming to see me, David sometimes felt that he was left out and was regarded as another carer rather than my husband and companion. He felt that he'd lost his identity and become an appendage to me. Unfortunately this was inevitable, the main focus of attention being on the disabled person.

Most people recognised David's worth and said to me

what a wonderful person he was. They realised how much he had given up to care for me and felt that I was lucky to have him. I agreed because without his love and support there were times when I would have given up. Without his love and willingness to care I would have had to live in an institution. Unfortunately, though I said these things to him, others rarely reinforced the massage.

The first week that I was home I felt quite tired. As I still had the pressure area on my thigh, I was quite happy to stay in bed. My bed faced a window which look out onto our veranda and a group of trees on the adjoining property. I could see birds and one day I saw a large cream and brown butterfly fluttering by in the sunlight. It was the first butterfly that I had seen in more than a year. The next week I became bored with lying in bed and tired of being in my nightwear all the time, so I decided to get dressed even if I spent the day in bed.

We made a trip to the local doctor so that I could introduce myself. As we had changed areas, I needed to find a new doctor and chose the one that Helen went to. He assured me that there was no need for surgery visits because he was happy to see me at home. I had mixed feelings about this as I knew that he normally only did home visits for a special reason. Though I wanted to be treated like other people I realised that my circumstances were somewhat different. Following this visit I was sitting outside the surgery talking to Helen's mother, Grace, when an overly-made-up elderly woman approached us.

'Oh you poor thing!' she exclaimed. 'Whatever happened to you?'

'I fell off my bike and broke my neck,' I replied.

'Oh, you poor thing. Will you always be like that?'

'Yes, my disability is permanent.'

'Oh, you poor thing. How are you?'

'I'm very well,' I replied firmly. 'How are you?'

'Not very well, I have this dreadful sciatic pain. It's absolute hell, I can tell you. I'm on the way to see the doctor now.' And with that she tottered off

Grace and I laughed about this exchange. No doubt I had made the woman's day because she had spoken to someone worse than herself. People's reactions to me varied but were generally friendly and helpful, however some people spoke to David or whoever else was with me and called me *she*. I found this objectionable. Though I was physically disabled, my other senses were not impaired. I could usually break down this barrier by asserting the right to speak for myself. Small children were frankly curious about me and the dials on the ventilator. As we were at eye level, I would smile and say hello. I did not mind being asked about my disability though I found it was rather tedious at times repeating the details of my accident.

David and I went out to restaurants several times with friends. The first time was a hassle because I had a blocked catheter. David had to change my clothes when he arrived home from work, so we were running late. The traffic was heavy and when we arrived parking was difficult. We found a ramp over the gutter so that I could drive along the pavement, but there was no such access at the other end, so we had to return to where we started from before driving off up the road. Friends helped me up the step into the restaurant, and once there we had an enjoyable meal.

Whenever we went out it was necessary to plan where we were going and to think about access. It would have been good if I had a lighter manual chair as there were some friends I could not visit because access was difficult. This chair had only been ordered shortly prior to my leaving hospital.

We went shopping and again looked for places where access was easy, and the aisles wide. This became easier as my wheelchair driving improved and I followed David around looking at things while he chose purchases according to his list. Our roles had reversed. Wherever possible we used disabled parking facilities when we went out. We were consistently surprised at the number of able-bodied people who also used these facilities even when there were empty spaces nearby.

One night at college where I'd resumed my studies, we were parked in by a man with paraplegia. If he'd taken the trouble to look, he would have seen the hoist on the back of the van and the disabled sticker on the windscreen. The guy arrived just as David had given up trying to manoeuvre the van out with the help of a student. The man agreed to move his car then looked at David and said rudely, 'What's wrong with you? You're not disabled.'

'No, I'm not,' David replied politely, 'but would you like to meet my wife?' He indicated towards me waiting patiently on the side of the road.

Just as frustrating were the people who parked across the access ramp at college even though it was clearly marked for use by the disabled and designated no standing. Often it meant that I or David had to ask people to move their car and sometimes wait until they were found. More often than not, the offending car was owned by one of the lecturers. The receptionists and security guards at college were particularly helpful in this regard.

After a week at home I returned to college to complete the Graduate Diploma in Administration which I'd been partway through when I had the accident. David had to accompany me and therefore drove me to college two nights a week and came to the lectures as my "minder". As the college was fairly new, access was relatively easy. But I tended to drive the chair too far into the lifts and kept banging my toes on the wall as I found it hard to judge where my feet where.

A friend jokingly suggested that I place a little red flag on a pole on the footplates so that I could tell where my toes were. However, after a few weeks my judgement improved, but one night while backing out of the lift I reversed into a wall and put a small hole in my ventilator tubing by catching it on the rough concrete. Fortunately I was only losing a small amount of air and we patched the hole with electrical tape until we could get replacement tubing. This took some time to arrive because the courier company could not find our address. Luckily the patch held. I had been sent home from hospital without any spare tubing.

Partly because the college had good access, there were a number of students in wheelchairs. Most of the staff were very willing to help people with special needs; this included the gatekeeper, security guards, receptionists, librarians as well as the teaching staff. All the lecturers asked me if I had any special requirements and I reassured them that I would ask for help if necessary. I did not want to be treated as someone special unless I ran into difficulties. I was determined to be a normal student and to complete the course using my academic abilities.

The ventilator was noisy and I knew that some of my fellow students found this distracting. People helped by opening doors and moving desks out of my way. I knew several of the students either through work or college and this helped me to feel more comfortable. Initially it was difficult returning to study after a year's break and the many changes brought about by my accident. In addition, I had to find new ways of doing things such as making notes when reading and including references when writing assignments. This would have been easier if I had been set up properly with the computer and page-turner. I asked my attendants to help me read. We worked out a system of recording page numbers and then typing notes and references into the computer.

My first assignment was the worst I had ever written and lacked references. I felt embarrassed about handing it in. Although the others were better, they were not up to my previous standard due to disruptions such as difficulty getting to lectures when David had the flu or I visited hospital. Using the library was also more difficult and David searched for books for me whereas previously I used to browse well beyond the recommended reading list.

We had a few dramas whilst living in Dire Straits which, though frightening at the time, we laughed about afterwards. Sometimes the ventilator tubing came adrift and the low-pressure alarm would sound indicating that I was not breathing. This happened once when Anomi had gone to the toilet. I was using the computer and she realised that things were serious when I did not answer her call of, 'Are you all right?' but dropped my mouth stick instead. She pulled up her knickers but came running in with her pants at half-mast to reconnect me.

'Can't even go to the toilet in peace,' she remarked.

On the way to college one afternoon, David had stopped at the lights on a dual carriageway and my tubing fell apart just as the lights turned green. David had to jump in the back of the van to reconnect me despite the abuse and angry honking of the drivers behind. I laughed at the time but apologised when I saw David's pale, sweaty face. Though I had accepted the inevitability of my own death and believed that I was living on borrowed time, for David and my carers it was a different matter. They felt responsible for keeping me alive even though I did not want to burden them with this responsibility.

We also had other laughs such as when one nurse put on David's gumboots to hand-ventilate me in the shower and the other nurse showering me accidentally filled her boots with water. Or the time when a man from Telecom came to look at the phones, but to get to the phone connection in the bedroom he had to crawl behind the back of my bed. Anomi arrived and was asking Trish and me how we were when his head popped up beside the bed.

'Are you keeping a man under the bed?' Anomi exclaimed in shocked surprise.

I also had dramas with the chair which weren't so funny. Swinging around the corner from the kitchen I put holes in the wall and at other times scraped doorways. Other people in wheelchairs reassured me that they did similar things which made me feel less of a disaster area, but it infuriated David. Welding on the chair also broke. This occurred to one of the leg-rests on a public holiday and we had to contact the NRMA road service who wired the pieces together until we could get it fixed properly.

More dramatically one day while in the van on the way to college, the whole back of the chair collapsed. We had no alternative but to return home but luckily, we had not gone far. Neighbours helped David unload me from the van and carry me bodily into the house. We then called Shaun to help get me into bed.

'Bloody hell!' exclaimed the technician who came to fix the chair the following day as he surveyed the damage. He replaced the back of the chair promptly which was good.

We also made alterations to the chin control which had a

convex metal fitting into which my chin was supposed to fit. I found the metal hard and tended to become sweaty so that I frequently slipped off. We solved this problem by padding the metal cup with a piece of foam and covering it with cloth. This made it much easier to drive. But added to this, the bar of the chin control tended to slip because the metal was too soft and tended to distort. This was a most annoying problem and one which we did not resolve until months later.

David made a lighter chest strap which fitted high under my arms, stopping me swaying from side to side in the van but failed to stop my arms from falling down the sides of the chair. This invariably happened in places where David could not stop easily such as when we were crossing Sydney Harbour Bridge in peak hour traffic. There were times when my shoulders became extremely sore.

I also had problems with my catheter because I had a urinary tract infection when I left hospital. This caused sediment to block the catheter. I went through a frustrating period of leaking around the catheter and putting up with wet pants. We asked the local doctor to prescribe antibiotics which eventually worked. There were also mechanical problems such as when one of my carers put my leg bag on upside down or the tap of the bag was not screwed up properly. We also found the valve into the bag clogged up after a while and disrupted the flow of urine. Eventually we sorted these problems out. Maureen had warned me that I might also have bowel accidents when I went home due to the change in diet. But apart from immediately after the enema, this did not occur in my case. With the increased fibre and fresh vegetables in my diet, I was able to reduce the amount of laxatives I was taking without any ill effects.

After returning home, the dressings on my pressure area was changed and both the nurses and I had high hopes the sore would heal quickly. It did so, albeit only slowly even though I spent large amounts of time in bed. Going to college and getting up at other times did not appear to have a detrimental effect on the healing process even though it was not the recommended way of treating a pressure area. I had no regrets about doing either because having spent such a long time in hospital unable to go anywhere, I was eager to get on with my life. The pressure area did break down once when I sat for too long in wet pants. Because we were at college, I was unwilling to return home and miss the lectures. It started to heal after that and became quite small. Then to everyone's surprise it broke down again after I had spent a week in bed. It was healing again when I returned to hospital.

In addition to the other dramas, we had a terrible hailstorm one day. Friends from Queensland were visiting us plus their grandmother who was in her nineties. It was a frightening experience as hail the size of tennis balls battered against the windows breaking one of them. David and Greg quickly erected a tarpaulin and fortunately not too much damage was done. I was concerned about my friend's grandmother who, as well as being elderly, was terrified of storms due to an experience that she had as a girl. Fortunately, we were able to reassure her and she returned home safely once the storm had passed.

Anomi was not so lucky. She'd left shortly before the storm started and was caught by it in her car at Regents Park. Terrified, she lay on the floor of her car as the hail battered against the glass and dented the bodywork. The following day when we went out, there were signs everywhere of the aftermath of the storm, broken windows, missing roof tiles and broken trees. Trish was unable to come to work as half her roof was gone and she had numerous windows broken at the back of her house. Many other people in the area had similar stories.

We took the opportunity during those months to catch up on all the social life that I had missed in hospital. I rang my sister and friends overseas. It was good to be able to talk directly to them. We invited friends around for dinner and had a barbecue in the garden one sunny weekend. We also visited friends even though the access was difficult sometimes, such as when we visited Peta's place. We took the portable ramps so that I could negotiate the steep driveway, drive along the veranda out onto the patio and up one step into the house. On my birthday we went to the Regent Hotel for a delightful lunch. I started to feel like a normal human being again. We also went to barbecues at the Paraquad Training Centre and got to know some of the other disabled residents. Often people assume that because you are disabled that you will immediately make friends with other such people. This is not necessarily true. Some we made friends with like Sam and Wanda and their two children, but others we had little in common with other than our disability.

Sam had injured his spine following an accident when he was driving a truck of hot bitumen. Just before the accident, his truck had a major overhaul, but the mechanic had failed to reconnect some of the suspension properly. When he was driving carefully around a sharp bend on a steep road, the connection came adrift. The truck rolled down an embankment onto the railway line and the trailer flipped over the cab pouring hot bitumen onto Sam. People at the scene of the accident managed to stop a high-speed passenger train a few yards from the truck. He is now a low-level quadriplegic.

Though Sam felt lucky to be alive, the accident had changed his life and that of his family. There were, for example, incredible strains on their marriage because among other things their house was not wheelchair accessible. This meant that Sam had to live apart from his family for two years before Berala was ready. In addition, they had constant battles with solicitors about settlement of the damages claim. It is little wonder that so many people split up when one partner becomes disabled.

David and I resumed our sex life though it was different because I could not feel David touching me nor could I put my arms around him or touch him. The thought of not experiencing an orgasm was devastating. I felt a dreadful emptiness. We both needed a lot of reassurance that what we were doing was pleasurable to the other. I remembered Noel's words that anything that was enjoyable to both parties was all right, but one needed to talk about their needs and possibly find new ways of doing things.

This was certainly true and patience plus a sense of humour helped. Now I experience an overall feeling of sexual wellbeing when we make love. For men who are paralysed, lovemaking may be more difficult but there are devices which enable them to have erections and to ejaculate. Most things are possible and I was not surprised when later I contacted Paul and Penny to hear that they had a baby girl.

I was in a quandary as to what to do about work because I was waiting to hear about the phrenic nerve stimulator plus I still had the pressure area. Though I was keen to return to work I did not want to start something and then have to stop halfway through. I did go into work several times and it felt good to be with my old team members again. Had we stayed in Sydney I would have recommenced running health education programs with Helen. I did give a talk on stress management to the community rehabilitation nurses group to which Annie and I belonged. It made me very aware of the noise of the ventilator and I looked forward to the time when I would be on the phrenic nerve stimulator.

In April, Professor Chalker rang me to say that approval for the phrenic nerve stimulator had been granted and parts had arrived from America. He sounded like a boy with a new toy. Though I was pleased by this news, I had very mixed feelings about returning to hospital. I was comfortable living in Dire Straits and had an established routine so that I did not have to ask to be showered, get my hair brushed or even ask for a cup of tea. I got on well with my attendants and the community nurses but continued to worry about the effect my disability was having on David's life. College kept me busy and stimulated and I worried that a lengthy stay in hospital would mean missing too many classes. In addition, I dreaded the thought of not being in control of my life and having to fit in with the hospital routine again. Poor David received the brunt of this and I became very snappy with him.

At the end of May I returned to hospital to have the phrenic nerve stimulator implanted.

Seven

Phrenic Nerve Stimulator

....

> *"We who have the karma to live,*
> *are both blessed and cursed without survival,"*
> *Cambodian survivor of the Pol Pot regime.*

'We can give you your old bed back,' the nurse said. I know that this was intended to make me feel at home, but I experienced a sinking feeling as I looked at the bed and the same boring wall opposite. I would rather have been by the window, though I did not really want to be there at all. The nurses, however, appeared pleased to see me and I began to feel guilty about my negative feelings. Many of the dressers expressed concern at seeing me back because such a return often meant that there were problems at home. But I was able to reassure them that everything was fine and that I'd returned for an operation. Many of the faces in the ward were the same, but there were some new ones, both nurses and patients, a mixture of the familiar and the different. It did not take long to get back into the ward routine but I looked forward to having the operation and returning home, and this time for good.

Dr Angelis had worked hard to coordinate everything. Dr Flecter and his surgical team were prepared for the operation the following week when a technician arriving from England to discuss the intricacies of the phrenic nerve stimulator. Dr Angelis brought her to meet me and I was able to ask questions as well as see the various parts of the stimulator before they were implanted. There were three parts. A cathode shaped like a small flat rubber arrow would be implanted over the phrenic nerves in the neck. These cathodes were connected by wires to two receivers; small plastic discs with wires and a smaller metal disc inside. All this was implanted under the skin of the chest.

On the outside was a transmitter, a small square metal box which had various dials and a battery. The transmitter was connected to the receivers via two wires that ended in rubber rings taped to the skin. It was somewhat like the early types of heart pacemakers that also had external components. Though this procedure had been used for several years in America and Sweden, I was to be the first in New South Wales. It would be done in two stages and was important that it be successful because if it helped me, it could help others.

For the first time since my accident, I was able to make a conscious choice as to whether I lived or died. Prior to this, I had felt very ambivalent about my survival, but now I decided

Seven   Phrenic Nerve Stimulator

that I wanted to live. Being in control of my life is very important to me.

Dr Angelis had tried to anticipate every eventuality but could not have anticipated a burst water main which cut the water supply to the operating theatre complex. The operation had been booked for early in the morning. It was delayed until eleven o'clock as everyone waited to see if the damage could be repaired quickly. Then the decision was taken to do the operation in another hospital. This meant transporting all the personnel involved plus their instruments and setting up in another operating theatre. I and the anaesthetic registrar were transported last.

'I don't know if you remember me,' said the registrar. 'I was in casualty when you were brought in on the day of your accident.'

I thought about asking whether it was he who passed the nasogastric tube, and if so he was the one who bought me back into the real world. I did not ask him however, because I was feeling anxious about the operation and shut thoughts of the accident from my mind.

Fortunately after such a disastrous start to the day everything went smoothly and the technician was impressed at how quickly Dr Flecter located the phrenic nerve. I awoke in recovery with a mildly sore neck and a surgical dressing under the right clavicle. The first operation was complete.

I then had to wait two weeks for the second operation. Risk of infection and consequent destruction of the phrenic nerve was the main complication of this operation, which is why one side is done at a time. I was placed on a high dose of antibiotics. Unfortunately, these exacerbated my skin rash and my itchy face drove me to despair.

The period following the operations was spent in bed. I passed the time writing assignments for college, trying to study and read but it was difficult. I had to fit in with the ward routine, but I needed help setting up my computer and to read. Though the ward was busy, some nurses were very helpful, but others would make me wait with precious hours ticking by. I found this very frustrating but chose to say nothing. Instead, I longed to go home where I had attendants who could help me. I was also missing college lectures. Though this was a worry, I could do nothing about it and hoped to catch up later.

After the stitches came out at the end of ten days, Dr Angelis and Lorrain tested the stimulator. We were all in a state of suspense, anxious to see if it worked. Dr Angelis taped the right electrode to my chest and connected it to the transmitter. Lorrain turned off the ventilator and we all held our breath as Dr Angelis turned the transmitter on. I felt my right diaphragm move; it felt very heavy and floppy and tongue-shaped, tapering toward the middle of my chest. I took several breaths before Dr Angelis turned the transmitter off and Lorrain put me back on the ventilator. It worked and we were thrilled. I looked forward impatiently to the next operation.

The day of the second operation came. I asked one of the nurses to suction me, which she started to do. But instead of the usual bullet on the tracheostomy tubing, I had a straight through connection which meant I lost air very quickly. Had the nurse replaced the cap on the tracheostomy when she found that the suction unit was not working there would have been no problem. However, she was so bothered by the suction unit that she omitted to do this, nor did she hear the ventilator alarm or my clicks for attention. After what seemed like an awfully long time when I was feeling very light-headed, Geoff left his patient to see what was wrong. He and the other nurses started hand-ventilating me. They gave me one suction and went to go down again. My whole world went black.

I woke to feel Meg's cool fingers on my forehead. They say that I had a respiratory arrest. All I know is that having so recently taken the decision to live, this incident frightened me severely and made me realise how vulnerable I was. Furthermore I worried that the operation would be postponed, but they took me to Recovery and kept me there for a couple of hours before proceeding with the operation. It was quite cold there and I was amused to see the labels "North Pole" and "South Pole" taped on the doors.

After the second operation, I had another ten days rest before the stitches came out. I was worried about the amount of college I was missing plus the difficulties I was experiencing referencing my assignments. When Dr Angelis offered to let me go home for ten days before starting the pacing program, I readily accepted even though I knew that I might have to wait for an empty bed before I could return. Going home enabled me to complete my assignments for the term with the assistance of my carers. I could also return to attending lectures two nights a week and did not feel that I was falling so far behind. In addition, I was longing to have a shower and to wash my hair which was unbearably greasy and scabby through not being washed.

There was something else that I had to sort out; my order for medical consumables through the government funded PADP scheme. Regina had advised me to contact the PADP clerks at my nearest centre as soon as possible after leaving hospital. However, a month passed before I contacted them and suggested that I meet them to discuss my needs. But there was a note of panic in the clerk's voice as she reassured me that all that was necessary was to fill out the requisite form, supply them with a prescription and a list of equipment. Then I discovered I had not been given a prescription when I'd been discharged and promptly contacted the hospital. When this arrived a week later, I filled in the form and sent it off with the prescription which listed the type and amount of aids that I needed for three months. Then I waited patiently.

I was rather surprised and irritated when three weeks later I received a letter from the clerks stating that they did not do three monthly orders, and could I supply them with a list for that month. A phone call would have been much quicker and cheaper. I had heard from other people that the clerks in this particular centre were difficult to deal with. Therefore, when I typed out a list I tried to make it as comprehensive as possible and included order numbers for everything except standard stock items such as packets of sterile gauze. *Pity the person with poor English skills*, I thought.

Two weeks later I rang them; the clerk was very officious and said that they'd received my order and they were processing it. She barely gave me time to speak and then cut the conversation short. This was particularly annoying as there are pauses and hesitations in my speech because I have to wait for the machine to give me the next breath in order to talk. Seeing how upset I was, Trish offered to contact them and I readily agreed. Trish continued to contact them on a regular basis to be greeted with promises that the order was being processed.

By this time we were becoming anxious as we were running low on stock, though the nurses kept us supplied with some things such as dressing packs. Then at the end of April, Trish was told that the order had not been processed because I was in hospital. I was furious and rang them to say that I was still at home and demanded to know who had told them otherwise. The clerk replied that it was the district nurse. As the nurse in question was on holiday, I could not verify this with her, but was puzzled why she should say such a thing. Finally when I was able to ask her about this I discovered there had been no such communication. When I was contacted by one of the clerks two days later to check all the items on the order, I realised that they'd not been processing the order at all. Two weeks later the order was ready and Trish went to pick it up. However, when we started putting it away we noticed that we had only received half the number of items we asked for. Some essential items such as humidifiers (which humidify and filter the air I breathe and which are changed daily) were missing. This time we had the district nurse ring to ask why the order was incomplete and the answer was that I was ordering too much stock.

'I only order what I need,' I exploded on hearing the news. 'Anyway, just who do they think they are? They are not nurses or doctors; they are clerks. They have never met me so how do they know what my needs are?'

The district nurse told them that all these supplies were necessary and needed urgently and the clerks promised to fill the complete order. We then contacted the clerks to ask about the order and especially the humidifiers. At this we were told that they had not supplied me with humidifiers because they were not a regular item and I'd not given the name of the supplier. I suggested they ring the Intensive Care unit of the major hospital in that area or Regina. So that something would be done quickly I contacted Regina myself. She gave me the hospital store's contact and from there I asked Anomi to take over as I was in the middle of writing a college assignment. Anomi then spent a frustrating morning trying to find the name of the supplier of the humidifiers but getting nowhere she was forced to give up. We then phoned Paul and Penelope who gave us the name of a supplier, and we passed this on to the clerks.

When we contacted the hospital about my return to start the pacing program, there was no bed available. However, I did not mind because this meant I could finish the last week of the college term before a two-week break. It would have been nice to have started the program during this period, but there was still no bed.

Meanwhile, most of the rest of the PADP supplies arrived but not the humidifiers and I was starting to feel desperate because I could not survive at home without them. Paul lent me some of his humidifiers until mine were replenished, but this meant that I would be constantly short each month. We also put in another order as the clerks had taken so long to do the last one. Naturally they protested. Another week passed and I returned to college; still no hospital bed. I was now impatient to start the pacing program.

'If a bed becomes available,' Trish said, 'I will go in there and lie on it and tell everyone it's occupied until you arrive.'

When we rang the following week, a bed was available, but then came a mad scramble to get there by eleven am. David had gone to work but came back to take me in rather than rely on access cabs which are frequently late. Anomi came over to give extra help. It had to be that morning I had a mucous plug in my lungs that kept setting the high-pressure alarm off on the ventilator. However, we made it in time.

The electrodes were taped over the receivers on my chest and connected to the transmitter. Then the ventilator was turned off and the transmitter turned on for three minutes. My pacing program had commenced. I started with three minutes per hour and this was gradually increased under Dr

Angelis's supervision to five minutes, then ten and so on. At first, three minutes seemed like a very long time and I felt tired and breathless at the end of it. I never knew breathing could be so stressful.

Dr Angelis and Lorrain checked my tidal volumes (the amount of air I breathe in) regularly and before each increase in the period of pacing. Naturally, all the nurses were very interested in my pacing program. Rita continued to make jokes about my transmitter by making telephone hand signs whenever she passed my bed. The other nurses would gather around my bed to watch me breathe. I felt it was a little like watching grass grow.

'Ooh, I can see your boobs shaking,' the young nurse remarked.

I laughed. 'Maybe I should purchase some brightly coloured tassels.'

Gradually the time increased to fifteen minutes then half an hour. I returned to college two nights a week and continued the pacing program there. When my time reached forty-five minutes then an hour, I took weekend leave and came home. But it was tiring for David and Anomi to be constantly switching me from one machine to another.

Both my return to college and weekend leave put a lot of stress on David because he had returned to work on a consultant basis rather than sitting at home being lonely. On college nights this meant that he had to leave work early in the afternoon, drive halfway across Sydney to pick me up then back across Sydney to

Seven Phrenic Nerve Stimulator

take me to college. He would then take me back to the hospital followed by an hour's journey home. On one of the college nights, he got home about midnight. Had I been able to take an access cab it would have meant that I could at least meet him at work which would have shortened his journey considerably. But this wasn't possible because I needed an escort and I could not use my care attendant hours while in hospital.

During this period I found being in hospital even more difficult. I had been there for two weeks when I had a confrontation with Geoff. This was over two issues which could have been avoided if the nurses had done as I requested. First, the electric bed which they put me in wasn't working properly and slowly but surely it ground to a halt. Though I repeatedly asked for it to be replaced nothing was done until one weekend it stopped working entirely. This meant that I could not sit up at all. The dressers did what they could by stuffing pillows behind the mattress, but this was far from satisfactory and my neck and back felt sore.

The other issue was that the cable which connected my ventilator plug to the battery on the chair had broken when staff were putting me into bed. This was serious as it meant that I could not get up and use my wheelchair for any longer than forty minutes, the amount of time the internal ventilator battery lasted. This meant that I had to stay in hospital, not going anywhere, so home or to college was out of the question. But as I had hoped to do both within the next few weeks, I wanted the cable repaired as quickly as possible. It was a simple matter of fusing two wires together, but again I was fobbed off with excuses. On the Monday morning I had enough and at the first opportunity, I tackled Geoff. Firstly, I asked him when they were going to replace the bed and pointed out that it was no longer working.

'Soon,' was the reply.

'When?' I asked. 'Today, tomorrow, next week, next month?'

Perhaps stung by my sarcasm, Geoff answered, 'You have to be patient. You are not the only one in here. Some of the others are very sick.'

'I've been patient,' I snapped. 'I have been bloody patient for two weeks and I am sick of putting up with a sore back and neck because of a bed that doesn't work.'

'Well, Mr Smith is going home today, and you could have his bed, but we can't do the changeover until after lunch.'

'That's all right, action at last. Also I want the cable to the ventilator battery repaired. It is just a simple matter and should only take you five minutes.'

'David should have repaired it before you came in.'

This was the last straw. 'It was broken after I came in here,' I exclaimed angrily. 'Your staff broke the cable and I want your staff to mend it. Besides, if the cable had been broken at home, I would have been unable to get in here. The journey takes over an hour and the internal battery only lasts forty minutes.'

The bed was changed that afternoon and the battery was repaired the following day. Later Geoff said to me, 'I don't know what you've done to the bed, but it's completely ruined now.'

As this remark was clearly ridiculous, I chose to ignore it.

It was unfair to make comparisons between home and hospital. At home I had one carer whereas in hospital there were two nurses in the acute section of the ward to six patients. However, at home I never had to ask for my face to be washed, my teeth to be cleaned or my hair to be brushed, but in hospital I had to and very often. Likewise, having a shower was never a part of my hospital routine and I always had to ask for one. Sometimes this was difficult because the ward was often very busy. I knew that some nurses would shower me if it were at all possible but with other nurses it was a waste of time asking them because they had different priorities. I asked them anyway because I resented depending on the willingness of some but not others. Going for four days without a shower was tolerable but longer periods than this and my scabby, itchy scalp drove me to distraction.

After one such extended period of eleven days and repeatedly asking to have my hair washed, I was in a state of frustration and despair. Meg who was working on night duty knew I was hanging out for a shower and asked me if I had one that day. I replied that I had not but then much to my chagrin burst into tears. The following morning Meg offered to shower me with the assistance of an enrolled nurse. She had just completed a long night and I did not expect her to stay back.

'You don't have to do that,' I replied.

'I know, but I want to,' she stated firmly.

Regina's permission had to be sought, and she was clearly not happy with this situation, but Meg was obviously determined to give me a shower. Regina came to see me to emphasise that this was a one-off occurrence, but I never expected it to be otherwise.

Following the shower, Meg said to me, 'Do you know that you are the only woman in the ward? Perhaps you should do a streak.'

I looked down at my skinny legs and fat belly. 'No, it would put them off their breakfast,' I laughingly re-joined.

I was not unduly concerned about the appearance of my body. After all, I was a middle-aged woman who had always been overweight, never conforming to the conventional ideal of feminine beauty. But I felt comfortable with my body. Had I been younger or more concerned about my image, then I would have found these changes very difficult to come to terms with.

Often, I had a dilemma between feeling empathy for the nurses who were rushed off their feet and asking them for things to be done. I was so physically dependent. My comfort depended very much on which nurses were on duty. Nurses such as Maureen would always ensure that I was comfortable, that I had something to do and that I had enough to drink. This latter was very important as I need to drink between two and three litres per day because of my indwelling catheter.

It was very frustrating on some days to be constantly told by the nurses that they would be 'back in a minute', or to wait to be given a drink. Worst of all were the nurses who gave me half a carton of juice and then put it down. I assumed that I had drunk all the juice only to find when David came that the carton was still half full and had been sitting on the locker all day.

'You haven't had enough to drink,' the night nurse would say accusingly. It was never for want of asking but rather the fact that I could not feed myself.

The other thing that really irritated me was that people never put things back in the same place twice. At home, I knew where my personal items were kept and could direct people where to find them. In hospital, we were constantly looking for hairbrushes, night splints and even the air-bag which was used in emergencies to hand-ventilate me.

Fortunately, not everything was negative and there were some lighter moments. Once the man in the bed next to me asked Helen if she was my mother, probably based on the observation that she was a regular visitor. As I am a few years older than Helen and have many more grey hairs, I remarked, 'I've heard of immaculate conception but this is ridiculous.' We had a good laugh about that.

Then I discovered that Rita's pet hate was cleaning patients' dentures and I asked Helen to give her a packet of lollies in the shape of teeth.

As the weeks went by, I found it more and more difficult to remain in the ward constantly surrounded by sick people and grieving relatives. As my pressure area had still not healed when I returned to hospital, I had agreed to stay in bed in the hope that it would do so. In order to overcome the problem of sore neck and shoulders, the dressers and I devised a system of half turns which we called "Malcolms" after another patient who also requested such turns. This seemed to work well for a while and coupled with use of the dressing I'd used at home and a paste, the sore healed for a day before starting to break down again. Or I think it healed. One nurse said it was healed but others said it was very small; all too confusing.

There was a man in the ward at this time who not only had a spinal injury but also brain damage. Consequently, he was very confused and kept trying to climb out of bed. Then he also started phoning his relatives, talking to them in a loud emotional fashion. When he rang them at four in the morning and talked at great length on high volume, I had enough. I felt psychologically traumatised and felt the need to escape from the ward whenever possible, pressure area or not. As well as two nights at college and weekend leave, I got up each afternoon so that I could go outside and visit the patients in the other end of the ward. At least we had more in common and I could talk with them.

My pacing program continued to progress well. Dr MacDonld and Dr Simpson did some more testing shortly after the pacing program began. Obviously, the testing could not be as definitive as previously because they could not place their probe directly over the nerve, but they seemed pleased with the result and I hoped it helped with their research.

Seven   Phrenic Nerve Stimulator

Gradually my pacing periods increased. Dr Angelis and Lorrain continued to test my tidal volumes regularly and used these readings as a guide when making decisions about increasing the pacing times. I also became much attuned to what my body could tolerate and if I felt mildly tired, or slightly breathless at the end, then I was increasing my pacing correctly. If I had difficulty completing the time due to breathlessness, excessive tiredness or had a muscular ache like a tight band around my chest, then I needed to reduce the period a little.

I had a setback in the program when I got the flu; pacing was like trying to breathe through a wet sponge. Dr Angelis advised me not to try any of this for two days. This rest helped considerably. I could then understand the advisability of retaining the tracheostomy even if a person was pacing twenty-four hours per day.

When I reached four and a half hours on the pacing program and a similar period off, I started to run out of hours in the day. I had been back in hospital for two months and found it increasingly difficult to be in the acute section of the ward, constantly surrounded by sick people. I longed to return home.

Work on our new house was progressing fast. David had gone down to Strathalbyn when I'd started the pacing program in hospital and returned with pictures of the house with the brickwork completed, the roof on, and work started on the internal fittings.

But time was running out. There were people I wanted

to see and things I wanted to do before we left Sydney. My mother also wanted to visit us before we moved and I felt that I was getting behind in my college studies. I asked Dr Angelis if I could go home even though I'd not reached the optimal number of hours on the pacing program. Dr Angelis agreed provided I return each week so that the tidal volume tests could continue. I quickly contacted my carers, the community nurses, and it was with a feeling of relief that I went home the following week. One thing was certain; I never wanted to see that bed again.

I was appreciative of all the hard work that everyone had put into my program. Firstly, to Dr Angelis and Professor Chalker for the submissions they wrote and the lobbying they did to get funding and permission for the phrenic nerve stimulator in the first place. Dr Flecter and his surgical team could not have been more helpful, despite the problem with the burst water main. The nursing staff had been both supportive and attentive especially during the early stages of the program when they were constantly switching me from one machine to the other. Add to that a special thanks to both Lorrain and Dr Angelis for their monitoring and help with my pacing program. No, it was not that I was ungrateful, it was just that I had enough of being in hospital.

Eight

Goodbyes

....

'The time has come,' the walrus said,
'To speak of many things.
Of shoes and ships and sealing wax,
of cabbages and kings.'
Lewis Carol

Time was indeed starting to run out. Building had started on the new house in March after a delay waiting for council approval. Now it was nearing completion. Earlier David had driven down to South Australia whenever I was in hospital. Firstly to look around and then buy land and talk with a builder. Then he made three trips while the house was being built. Each time he made the long journey on his own and he would return looking tired but with photos and video of the progress. We would then discuss the next decisions which had to be made.

David bought back samples of bricks and tiles, but he would much rather that I had been there to share these decisions. Every time he travelled to Strathalbyn, I wished desperately that I could travel with him and share the driving and provide companionship. We both felt very lonely. I also worried he might have an accident while driving such long distances on his own. If he met with an accident there would be little that I could do to help and if he were killed what would happen to me? I would lie awake and worry.

Fortunately, when he got to Adelaide he was able to stay with our young friends Chris and Susanne and I knew that they would look after him. They had also helped us by searching for information on suitable house plans, visiting the site while building was in progress and purchasing garden equipment. David also took down a couple of precious plants which they took care of for us.

In September David flew over to make a final inspection of the house and accept the keys from the builder. During this time Helen stayed with me for the weekend and though David was anxious about leaving me, we had no dramas. The pair of us did, however, eat all the chocolate brownies which he had baked before he left, much to his disgust. We then had to decide when to move and chose a date in mid-October. But there was so much to organise. In the meantime, Chris and Susanne agreed to keep an eye on the house but we had no problems with break-ins or vandals.

When I returned home from hospital I wanted to make up for lost time. It was David's birthday in August, and I invited some close friends around for lunch. So that David did not have a lot of work to do, they all brought a plate and Helen made a chocolate cake in the shape of a teddy bear. On looking around the group, I thought what good friends they'd all been and how much I was going to miss them. We saw each other as much as possible over the next few weeks but we grieved over the forthcoming parting, so much so that David worried that I'd change my mind about moving.

On the contrary, I was looking forward to us being able to finally start a new life together and I had all sorts of plans. Yet at the same time, I was saying a final goodbye to my old life and feeling sad that my friends could not come with me. I knew that we would keep in touch and hoped that I would see some of them in our new home.

My mother came down to stay for a couple of weeks, and this time I was determined that we should go out and do things together. This we did, but we were both surprised and disappointed when we went to Bicentennial Park for a picnic to discover that the picnic areas were inaccessible because there were no gutter ramps. Nor could I go on the boardwalk to look at the mangroves because there were steps. It was very disappointing and we took our picnic elsewhere. After this, we went out to a variety of places with my mother and with friends. Meg came to lunch with us one day and I gave her a bag of purple jellybeans to remind her of all the times I had gone blue when she was caring for me.

Of course, all this sitting up did not do my pressure area any good and it started to break down again. This was the only time that I deliberately gave up on the pressure area when it was getting worse. But being able to say goodbye to my friends was far more important than the healing process. Besides, I felt that I would have plenty of time for healing when we arrived in Strathalbyn. Unfortunately, none of us took much notice of the hard lump, the size of a pigeon's egg, which Trish felt under my skin near the sore the day after I arrived home from hospital. Had I been aware of the implication of this I would have been more concerned.

My youngest brother sent me a set of tapes and a video on self-healing with a letter and stories about people who had recovered from spinal injuries. Though I knew he meant well I felt very angry. After all I had taught stress management for a number of years and was familiar with self-healing techniques. Did he think that I had not tried them? I'd in fact used them in those first few weeks following my accident, but they had not worked for me. If they had, I would be able to breathe and use my hands. Did that mean that I was a failure? I thought not. As for recovery from spinal injury, some people with incomplete lesions do sometimes improve, even several years later. But this was not the case where the lesion was complete. My disability was permanent.

'I can accept my disability, why can't he?' I complained to David.

'Means well,' he replied.

I acknowledged this, but it still took several months before I felt that I could listen to the tapes. When I did, I felt that some of the information wasn't appropriate for people with spinal injuries. For example, it is hard to be told to feel different parts of your body when you feel nothing. Unfortunately, such inappropriate gestures, though well-meaning, may add to the stress rather than relieving it.

On another front, the battle for the supply of humidifiers and other equipment continued. By now I was thoroughly fed up and wrote a blistering letter of complaint to the person in charge of the scheme at Head Office of the Department of Health. I do not know if this had the desired effect, but we received a phone call from the clerks the following week asking why we had not picked up the humidifiers as they had been ready for collection for a month. I felt very cynical about this as the humidifiers had not been ready the previous week when Trish rang.

My next order was processed fairly quickly, but it still necessitated Trish making three trips to collect the entire order. This annoyed me still further because my attendant care hours were limited and I could not afford to have them wasted in this way. In addition, Trish was often refused permission to park in the hospital grounds. This meant that she had to make several walking trips, sometimes blocks away, carrying heavy cardboard boxes. I knew that the administration of the PADP scheme varied from area to area and that much depended on the clerks who were employed. It was a pity, I thought, that all clerks were not like the one who worked in the health area with which I was involved. She was courteous, efficient and caring. I guess it is a question of attitude as to whether you see your clients as consumers of a service or whether you see clients as nuisances using up scarce resources. Few, if any, wish to be disabled and I certainly never asked for things which I did not need or could not use.

All my attendant carers had decided to remain with me despite my lengthy stay in hospital. I was both surprised and pleased by their loyalty because I did not relish the thought of finding new carers. I had heard of one man who'd signed himself out of hospital rather than lose his regular attendants. However, Trish and Anomi had taken other work while I was away but were pleased to come back, even though it would not be long before the move to Strathalbyn. Trish was pregnant and I had worried about her having to lift me, even though this was minimal risk in the first three months of her pregnancy. However, she was a sensible woman and this was not her first child, so I felt that the decision was hers. She remained healthy throughout her pregnancy.

There seemed to be such a lot to organise with the move from Sydney. We decided to use professional removalists rather than David having the huge chore of packing and unpacking. We got a couple of quotes but decided to send the cat down by air. The poor thing had just settled in and was to be uprooted yet again.

I asked that my attendant care scheme be transferred and was furious when told that this was not possible. When I had applied for and also when I'd been granted the scheme, I asked several people to check that it was transferable. Each time the answer had been yes, and this influenced our decision to move. We couldn't believe the scheme was not transferable and we wrote a letter to the minister. After a few weeks' delay, we received quite a pleasant letter from him saying that the scheme had been allocated to me personally no matter where I chose to live in Australia

After this it took a few more weeks for Paraquad to sort things out and contact their counterpart in Adelaide. So, it was with relief that I received a phone call from the coordinator of personal care services in South Australia introducing herself and asking a little about me. Within a week she had lined up a care attendant and arranged a time for us to meet after we had moved into our new house. I was impressed by her efficiency.

Elsewhere being transferred between spinal units was straightforward with Dr Angelis sending all the relevant papers to the director of the unit in Adelaide. The nursing service referred me to the district nursing service in South Australia. But here there was a bit of a worry because the nurses said that they could not come on the first day while we stayed in a motel in Adelaide, however this was soon sorted out. We decided to make three stops on the way over and David rang several motels to find ones that were suitable. He had a mixed response. Some people were extremely helpful and went to check that we could fit the hoist under the bed, but one person was quite rude, clearly not wanting to know us. Unfortunately much of this arranging had to be left to David, further adding to his workload.

I had resumed college while still in hospital and was very conscious of the number of lectures that I'd missed. In addition, we would be moving before the end of term and would miss the last few weeks. Fortunately I was allowed to do this, however I was determined not to miss any more lectures and worked hard to finish my assignments. When we left in October, I only had two assignments left to write. I felt proud that I'd been able to complete the year without needing to ask for any special favours despite the disruption my readmissions to hospital had caused.

David enabled me to attend college by driving me up there and sitting with me through my lectures. He also got books for me as well as giving me considerable support and encouragement. My care attendants also helped with reading and finding references. Without their help, I could not have completed the course. All my lecturers took an interest in what I was doing and wished us well when the time came for us to leave. I felt a little sad when we said goodbye knowing that I would probably never see them or my fellow students again.

We both wondered what we would do in the future and how we would occupy our time in Strathalbyn. We had plans for making a garden and talked of other things that we might do. I wanted to upgrade our computer in anticipation of being able to use this expanded capacity to help us find work.

At the suggestion of one of the therapists, I put in a submission for a computer and printer to the Commonwealth Rehabilitation Service. But the CRS wanted me to write to various services, asking if they were willing to employ me before they would consider my submission. I drafted a letter but never sent it. How could I? With my disability, any prospective employer would want to meet me first, and besides I was not familiar with the services in that area. I felt it better to wait until we had settled into our new home. Then I could meet people face to face and talk to them about what I had to offer. So instead of asking the Commonwealth Rehabilitation Service to purchase a computer for me, I asked the people who were in charge of my trust fund to buy one.

This fund had been set up by my colleagues at work. They had been busy raising money through things such as lamington cake sales and bush dances. They'd also had a very successful raffle of a beautiful patchwork quilt donated by one of the doctor's wives. We used this fund to buy the extra things we needed, things we could not have bought otherwise.

In October I went back into work for the last time. Anomi and I caught an access cab. This was the third time that I had caught such cabs and contrary to some other people's experience the cabs arrived on time, the drivers courteous and helpful. This driver looked rather rough and ready with a large beer gut and wearing shorts and thongs. But as we got talking, we realised what a nice, caring guy he was. When we started talking about attitudes toward people with disabilities, he told us a story.

He was parked one day at a taxi rank waiting to pick up an ordinary fare as he had no other work. A woman came along, took one look at his taxi and declared loudly, 'I'm not travelling in that!'

'Why not, lady?' the driver had asked, window down.

'Germs, germs!' she exclaimed, wildly arms waving.

'Don't worry, lady,' he replied, 'you don't have to travel with me. Wouldn't like you passing on your germs to any of my regular passengers.'

We both laughed and congratulated the driver on dealing with the situation so well. Later I felt very sad on arriving at work knowing that I would never pass that way again. Both Helen and I cried as we packed up my books and sorted through papers. Work had always been important to me and I had worked all my adult life except for periods when I travelled and a year off to go to college. In addition, I'd really enjoyed working with the rehabilitation team. Everyone had been very supportive following my accident. For a long time I had clung on to the impossible hope that I would be able to return in some capacity. It was a very big disappointment that I had not been able to do so.

All too soon it was time for everyone to go home and I said goodbye to the secretaries and to some of the therapists. Everyone else I would see at the weekend as the staff had decided to have a big farewell party for me at Peta's place. This time we took the manual wheelchair which made getting into their house much easier than the previous occasion. We had a wonderful day sitting in the sun, talking, eating and drinking. Coral's husband took a video of the day so as to have a record of the event. Whenever I look at it now, it brings back some very treasured memories. Then it was time to say goodbye; I would miss them dreadfully.

During this period, I continued to increase my pacing time. Initially Dr Angelis asked us to attend the hospital outpatients each week so that she and Lorrain could continue the testing. However, it was a hassle trying to get over there late in the mornings. As Lorrain was attending college once a week near to where we were living, it was decided that she could come to our place to do the testing. Everything continued to go well. I could pace for a large part of the day and paced when I went to college. I continued to increase my pacing time by half to one hour per week.

Two weeks before we left Sydney, I went to see Dr Angelis for the final time and a last change of the stimulator settings. As the testing was fairly rigorous that day, I was not surprised that I felt very tired and asked to be put back on the ventilator when the testing was completed. However, I was concerned when I was up in my chair two days later to find that after a couple of hours I felt tired, nauseous and headachy. I contacted Dr Angelis who advised me that these settings were very different from the previous ones but that they were the correct settings for me.

I persisted for another week but could not pace for longer than an hour or two when sitting in my chair. Something was wrong and I contacted Dr Angelis again, but she advised me to continue saying that these settings would take time to adjust to and that they were the optimum settings for me. I began to wonder whether other things were causing problems because I'd noted that I was more likely to suffer from physical symptoms when on the stimulator. *Could be the stress of moving*, I thought, *or the pressure sore causing me problems.* Once we left Sydney, I promised myself that I would increase my pacing hours.

Our last few weeks in Sydney had come all too soon in some ways and in others not soon enough. I had a chance to do most of the things I wanted and had said goodbye to most of my friends. A pity I would miss the last few weeks of college, but had been there for enough of the term to complete my last two assignments. We had dinner with Amy, Rolland, Lea and another friend. As I kissed them goodbye, I thought about what good friends and wonderful support they had been, not just to me but to David too. I had to say goodbye to Shaun too because he had another permanent job. Though I was sorry to see him go, I did not worry about other people coming from Home Care. It was only to be for a few weeks. I didn't worry, that is until I met Heidi, the new attendant.

Though a kind and well-meaning woman, the fact that I was on a ventilator seemed to send her into a panic. So instead of taking time to think before attending to me, she would rush at everything. Consequently, she frequently pulled on my ventilator tubing which then fell apart. But instead of reconnecting everything as soon as possible she would look at David in pure panic.

'Ah!' she would exclaim throwing the tubing up in the air before rushing from the room.

Because there was so little time left, we decided not to ask for another attendant hoping that she would learn to relax and do things properly, but she never did. In order to avoid the frequent sore throats which the wrenching on my tubing caused, I usually asked David to take care of it. Two nights before we left, Heidi really got on my wrong side in both senses when without warning she suddenly sat me forward. My ventilator tubing was still attached to the chair, and I could see it being stretched to its furthest limit before it thankfully fell apart.

'It's pulling on my neck,' I managed to croak.

It felt like my throat was being pulled out. I was not surprised that my throat was bleeding and I could barely talk the next morning. In fact, I felt so traumatised that I asked her not to undress me the following night but asked Helen to help instead.

There were a lot of last-minute arrangements. David and I both felt stressed but looked forward to the day when we would leave. Hopefully everything would be completed by then. We had put in my equipment order for the month of October weeks previously, but as usual, there were delays and we were worried about whether it would arrive before we left Sydney. The last thing that we wanted was to be organising supplies the minute we arrived. Trish by this stage was thoroughly frustrated with trying to deal with the PADP clerks and the district nurses contacted them on my behalf. This still necessitated phoning them on average twice a week to find out when the supplies would be ready and confirming that I did need all and everything. The nurses also found dealing with the clerks as frustrating. The supplies arrived in dribs-and-drabs. I never received my complete order.

By now Trish was obviously pregnant and finally the clerks allowed her to either park in the hospital grounds and or provide her with a shopping trolley in which to carry the boxes. They even offered to deliver the order which surprised us because they'd always maintained that no such service was available. But when the order did not arrive as promised, we contacted them yet again. At this we were told that the wrong address had been given, but when we checked it was correct. On further questioning we discovered that the driver had gone to a two-story house which was occupied by an Arabic speaking family.

Despite this being clearly not where I lived, the clerks continued to maintain that this was the address that I had given.. When Trish went to pick up the final order the clerks had heard on the grapevine that I was leaving.

'I am glad that Hilary is leaving because then she won't have to put up with people like you anymore,' Trish had told them.

She reflected not only my feelings but also the feelings of everyone who had the misfortune of dealing with these people. Through their procrastinations they may have saved a small amount of money by not supplying me with all the aids that I needed. Through their negative attitude, their rudeness, their constant questioning of my needs and their outright lies, they'd caused me a lot of hassles. Living with a disability is hard enough in itself. By not having orders ready on time or only having part of an order ready, the clerks made their own jobs more difficult and wasted a considerable amount of time and money through unnecessary phone calls and dealing with angry and frustrated clients.

David had his last day at work. It was as difficult for him to give up work as it had been for me. So much of ourselves is tied up in the work we do and how we see ourselves. He had given up so much to care for me, a well-paid job and career, his home in Sydney and a whole lifestyle. Often, I felt that it would have been better if I had died on that fateful day so that he did not have to make so many sacrifices. It is easy to say don't feel guilty about this, but I did for a long, long time. With David giving up work we were now totally reliant on my pension, and wondering how we would manage.

We also wondered what we would do in Strathalbyn. David planned to establish a garden and that would occupy him for a while but what would I do? My college course was finishing and I was writing this book. Would I be able to continue counselling and give talks to people? Before when I had gone to live in new places, I had been confident of my own skills and abilities and always looked forward to the challenge of making a new life and meeting new people. Now I was disabled and had lost many of my skills, would people think me incapable of doing things? I hated the thought of being housebound with nothing useful to do. Having both lived in country towns as children, David and I realised that it would take us a while to settle into Strathalbyn and get to know people. We felt both apprehensive about moving but eager to start a new life.

Two days before we were due to leave, the cat was picked up. He was placed in a cage and was on his way to the airport before he realised what was happening. Then he was flown over to Adelaide and boarded for a few days until we moved into the house. The packers arrived and packed everything except the clothes we were taking with us, the hoist, the commode chair, my ripple mattress, the suction units and a bucket and bowl. I no longer travel light these days. They packed the entire contents of our house in a few hours.

We moved out of the house that day. As I drove out of Dire Straits in my wheelchair toward the training centre where we would spend the next two nights, I thought it had been good living there. It had given us the opportunity to sort out our lives before making any final moves. In some ways, I would miss it. I would certainly miss my care attendants and Sam and Wanda with whom we had become quite friendly. The removalists arrived the following day and in contrast to the packers, they seemed to take the best part of the day to load all our belongings, but everything was packed very well. Eventually they finished and the truck left. Both Amy and Helen came to say goodbye which was painful for all of us. However, I knew that we would always be friends no matter where we lived.

The last day had arrived. Trish came early to give me

breakfast and help with the shower. We had asked Trish and Anomi to give the house a final clean. Anomi arrived later with a broom, a bucket and some cleaning material.

'As there's a petrol strike on, I thought I'd come by an alternative means of transport,' she said. 'I brought the bucket in case I got caught short on the way,' she added. Trish and I burst out laughing.

David packed the van then loaded me on. We said our goodbyes.

'I wonder if you'll have two crazy ladies like us to look after you,' Trish remarked, as she waved us off.

I wondered too. They had looked after me well and had been fun to be with. I cried a little as we left Sydney. In many ways I felt relieved that we were on our way and looked forward to seeing our new home. We were on our way at last. I had hoped to pace while travelling, but to my surprise, after an hour I felt so nauseated that I had to ask David to put me back on the ventilator. This was very disappointing as I'd hoped to resume my normal pacing hours. I put the nausea down to the fact that I was sitting on the pressure area which had deteriorated yet again.

Apart from a flat tyre, the trip was uneventful. We made the trip in fairly short stages and stayed in motels at Wagga and Mildura. Annie and her husband met us on the first night, and after a very pleasant meal with them, Annie helped David put me to bed. They returned in the morning to help get me up.

David then had to manage me on his own the next night

which was not easy after a long day's drive. Often, he had to stop to reposition me as I still tended to fall to one side despite the chest strap. Another problem which we had not yet resolved was that my arms kept falling off the armrests. I was thankful that I had brought a special strap which I wore while we drove along. This gave my shoulders good support, and they did not get sore on the trip.

With the need to do all the driving plus care for me, they were long days for David. Though I was doing nothing other than sit, I was also tired at the end of each day. It was a relief to arrive at our young friends Barry and Susanne's place in time for lunch on the third day. We were both exhausted.

Nine

Expectations and Disappointments

We stayed in a motel for two days waiting for our furniture to be delivered and unpacked before moving into our new home. Despite all David's concerns that I may not like the house, I loved it. I had seen so many pictures that it was exactly like I expected it to be. The house was very open plan and gave me easy access to most rooms. It also had lots of north-facing windows. This made it not only light and airy but also warm in winter. David had arranged for gravel to be placed on the drive and pathway so I could drive my chair in the front door. That felt really good.

Though the removalists had put things where we wanted, David still had the job of putting everything in cupboards, hanging pictures and generally organising stuff. Again I wished that I could have helped him, especially as we were still both very tired from our trip. David also collected the cat a few days later. He again went through a period of hiding in the cupboard and for months afterwards was reluctant to go out. The poor thing; he had turned into a narcotic closet cat.

Two days after we had moved, the coordinator of personal care services came to meet us and introduced us to Lillian who became my first new attendant carer. I liked her immediately and we had a lot in common as Lillian was a weaver as well as having had experience working with people with disabilities.

Over the following week I met two other carers. Ingrid was a keen gardener and worked in the local nursing home as well as with me. She and her husband had a property not far from Strathalbyn where they grew lucerne. Angela was an enrolled nurse and had worked in the local hospital for many years until she developed a back problem and had to give up nursing. She had a large family which she took care of and sometimes minded her grandchildren. She lives locally and does not mind if we call her when we need extra help at odd hours. It was good to get my care organised so quickly and without a lot of fuss.

The district nurses also started coming to attend to my personal care including dressings to my pressure area five days a week. With all these new people coming it meant extra work for David on top of everything else. He had to explain how my ventilator and the phrenic nerve stimulator worked and how to switch me from one machine to the other. He showed people the procedure for suctioning as well as many other things regarding my care. Little wonder that the poor man was

Nine Expectations and Disappointments

tired. When we had been in Strathalbyn a couple of months, we gave a talk to the district nurses about the various aspects of my care. This went very well and they later published my notes in their magazine.

We also met with one of the local doctors and joined the ambulance fund. As soon as possible we arranged to go to the spinal unit where we met Dr De Maria and Connie, the social worker. As we talked, I felt confident that I would be well cared for. A few weeks after this visit Dr De Maria and her team came to see us at home so that they could see where and how we lived and discussed some of the problems we had. There seemed to be so many things to organise such as where to get equipment and which service supplied what.

Earlier we had asked a couple of people to check on this before deciding to move to South Australia. The first reply was so vague that it was of no use and the other person gave us wrong information. We now found that the South Australian health service had different guidelines for health care; I was no longer eligible for PADP funding. Fortunately, the nurses could supply most things through the Domiciliary Care Scheme but tracheostomy items, which are both the most essential and expensive, we would have to buy ourselves. Fortunately, there was a fund which provided us with some financial assistance for these things but finding the money for the rest was a real worry. The equipment officer at the spinal unit did the ordering for me and it was a pleasure to deal with someone who ordered the equipment and consumables I needed without any fuss.

It was not going to be easy living on a pension. Connie advised us that we could apply for a part invalid pension and a carer's pension now that David was no longer working. This required filling out numerous forms and visiting the Social Security office. There we had to wait for several hours until dangerously close to closing time before being seen. Connie continued to help us by contacting the Social Security offices until my pension was approved.

Having worked all my adult life, I hated the thought of being reliant on benefits, but it was the only way that we could survive financially. It was also hard for David because initially, he was not considered eligible for a carer's pension despite the fact that he cared for me a hundred and forty-four hours per week. This saved the government tens of thousands of dollars which it would cost if I were in hospital or a nursing home. For some months all he received was the Domiciliary Nursing Care Benefit; other than that he had no income whatsoever. Later he was granted a part carer's pension. But as my invalid pension was reduced when this happened, financially we were not much better off. It seemed ironic that other people were paid to care for me and though David had more than a full-time job, in adding to this all he received was three dollars a day.

Shortly after arriving in Strathalbyn my father died. He was eighty-two years old and had been in hospital with a chest infection. My mother had visited him the day before and he was cheerful and looking forward to returning home the following day. Though I had little contact with my father in the

Nine Expectations and Disappointments

latter years of his life, under normal circumstances I would have gone to his funeral. However, the trip to Adelaide had exhausted both David and myself. Flying to Queensland was out of the question even if we could have afforded it. I would have liked to have been with my mother at this time to offer her support and comfort and I felt upset that this was not possible. We kept in touch though by phone and letters and I was glad that my brothers flew up there to be with her.

With all the sitting up and travelling, my pressure area had broken down again. As the nurses applied dressings to clean the wound, they probed deeper and discovered an area of calcified tissue. Was this the hard lump, I wondered, that Trish had felt under my skin when I came out of hospital? Though I was spending nearly all my time in bed and the nurses were dressing it daily, the wound became bigger and bigger. Whenever I got up in the chair, which was rarely, I felt nauseated. The wound started to weep copiously and worse still it started to have an offensive smell. My flesh was rotting and I felt disgusting. I knew that I would have to talk to Dr De Maria about my pressure sore and this would probably result in another admission to hospital. But first I had a wedding to go to.

Barry and Susanne had delayed the date of their wedding until I was in Adelaide and able to attend. I was not going to miss it for anything. On a cool but sunny day in November, David and I plus a friend from Perth made the trip to the church in the city. I was able to use a side entrance which had a ramp. Susanne, like most brides, looked beautiful with a garland of rose-buds in her hair. Barry looked very smart but serious in a dark suit. We enjoyed the ceremony which went without a hitch. David took a video.

Outside the church we congratulated the newlyweds and chatted with their parents and friends. After scattering them with rose petals we were soon all driving up into the Adelaide Hills for the reception at a golf club. I had to be carried up the flight of stairs to the dining area, but this was not a problem as there were many willing helpers. After a very pleasant meal and many toasts to the bride and groom we saw the young couple off. Then a number of us went to Susanne's parents for coffee and cake. What an enjoyable day it was.

The biggest disappointment about the deterioration of my pressure area was that except for a few special occasions, I was housebound. This made it almost impossible for us to meet new people. Shortly after we moved in, we had met one of our neighbours who invited us to help ourselves to their rainwater. We greatly appreciated this as the mains tap water tasted terrible. David started work creating a garden and planted trees and flowers at the front of the house. Barry and Susanne helped him make raised beds in which to grow vegetables. David did get talking to a few people when out working in the garden. One of the nurses also introduced me to Yvonne, a retired nurse who was very actively involved in the local community. Apart from these contacts, our social life was very restricted and I missed my friends. Even though they rang me and wrote letters, it was not the same as being with them.

Nine Expectations and Disappointments

Lillian said that she would help in whatever way she could and she lent me her crystal in order to give me healing energy. I hesitated about confiding in her however, because I felt I did not know her well enough yet.

I felt increasingly unwell, tired and nauseous most of the time. David and I started to fight with each other frequently and I became very depressed. Things were just not working out the way that I had hoped. I even contemplated suicide not because I particularly wanted to die but rather because I felt trapped by the whole situation. If I could not live at home, then the only alternative was for me to live in an institution which I did not want to do. The pressure area seemed to get bigger and bigger. I woke one night in a panic.

'They will put me in hospital,' I said to myself.

'They cannot make you do anything against your will,' I reasoned. 'But given the size of the pressure sore and the way things are going you had better ring Dr De Maria soon.'

'I don't want to go into hospital again,' I wailed. *You will have to if you are ever to get rid of this pressure area,* I said to myself and decided to contact Dr De Maria.

The district nurses were also concerned about the deterioration in the pressure sore and suggested contacting the local doctor. This we did and he felt that admission to hospital and possibly plastic surgery would be necessary. David contacted Dr De Maria on my behalf and we went to see her. I was admitted immediately, but unlike my previous admissions to hospital, I was placed in the rehabilitation section rather than the acute ward. The relief of not being surrounded by sick and recently traumatised patients was overwhelming. I was sufficiently close to the nurse's station that they could hear the ventilator alarms and I had a bell which I could press with my head when I wanted help. For most of the time I was there, I had a room to myself and other things were different too.

'How often do you normally have a shower?' the nurse asked.

This question was unexpected because I did not think that I would be allowed up for a shower with such a large pressure area. I soon discovered that the rehabilitation centre (and later the hospital) used a trolley with a special rubber mat to shower patients. This meant that you could be showered lying flat. What a vast improvement on all the rigmarole and hassle that I had gone through in Sydney trying to get my hair washed. What a relief to not have to ask to have my hair washed for it became a part of my routine care.

The orderlies came to turn me. 'Have you got any sore spots? How are your shoulders?' they asked. Again, I was surprised when I thought about all the times that I had complained of sore shoulders last time I was in hospital and had felt that I was talking to myself. Every time the orderlies turned me, they took the time and the care to position me correctly and neither my neck nor shoulders became excessively painful. This was a great relief because it had been a problem when I had been in hospital previously, especially when I was spending long periods on my side.

Nine Expectations and Disappointments

There were some things I did not like. Whenever the high-pressure alarm went off on the ventilator, some of the nurses felt obliged to move my tubing in case it was kinked. This rarely happened, and the alarm usually went off because I needed suctioning due to a build-up of secretions in my lungs. Moving my tubing was the quickest way I knew to get a very sore throat and I asked the nurses not to do this.

I liked my ventilator tubing to be pinned beside me so that the tubing was slack and I could move my head freely. Some of the nurses would tie it so that the tubing was taut and dragging on my neck or worse still, placed beside my ear where the noise of my respiration would drive me mad. Likewise, many of the nurses, unused to phrenic nerve stimulators, would drape my antennae wires either side of my head where they would catch around my ears. I sounded like a cracked record.

'Don't move the tubing. It's not kinked. I need a suction. Loosen the tubing off; it's dragging on my neck. And take it away from my ear, it drives me mad having it there. Put the wires under my nightie. Don't take them up round my head. They stimulate my diaphragm, not my brain,' and so on.

Then other things caused me considerable anxiety. 'Where do I disconnect you?' the nurses asked the first time they suctioned me. At this I had to hastily explain that this was not necessary and all they had to do was open the cap on the elbow connection on the ventilator tubing. A normal routine for anyone in my situation.

But following my experience of a respiratory arrest in

Sydney, I was likely to panic if anyone disconnected my tubing unexpectedly. Unused to doing tracheal suctioning, some nurses did not pass the catheter down far enough, and this was frustrating because I could still feel the mucous there. Of even greater concern were the nurses who did not switch me from the ventilator to the stimulator correctly or vice versa. The majority of nurses correctly connected me to both machines by switching the machine that I was going to use on first and then the other one off. And all this prior to disconnecting any tubes or leads. However, there were always exceptions.

'Would you put me on the ventilator?' I asked.

The nurse picked up my antennae leads. 'I can disconnect these now?' she asked.

'No, not yet,' I replied in alarm. 'You have to put me on the other machine first.'

'But I can disconnect these now?' she persisted.

'No, no, I can't breathe if you do that.' I would start to panic.

Was she listening to what I said? Would she disconnect me and walk away, inadvertently leaving me to die? I felt an overwhelming relief when she finally did as I asked. However, when we had a similar conversation a few days later, I felt that it was safer not to use the stimulator when she was on duty. Unfortunately, I had a few other such scares mostly because the nurse concerned was in a hurry and/or did not listen to what I said. Nor did I ever get used to all the lights being switched on when the staff came to turn me during the night. I can sleep or doze through most things but having bright

Nine   Expectations and Disappointments

lights shone in my eyes woke me up and I usually took a while to go back to sleep. Consequently, I slept badly and developed poor sleeping patterns.

After a few days I met Dr Morris, the plastic surgeon and a very likeable man. He prescribed treatment to clean the pressure area and agreed to operate on it after Christmas. This would mean lying in bed and being nursed from side to side for six weeks following the operation. However, I was willing to do this if it meant getting rid of the pressure area once and for all. For far too long it had been the bane of my life and had prevented me from doing the things I wanted to. I had started on tablets to replace some of the vitamins and electrolytes that I had lost through having such a large open wound. The dietitian also came to see me about eating a high protein diet. I rapidly started to feel better, and once the wound was clean, I was allowed up for two hours per day. This meant that I could have lunch with the other patients, and I could sit in the garden afterwards.

Some of the nurses and orderlies helped me pick roses from the garden. Though the gardeners were aware that patients and staff picked the flowers, we acted like naughty school children, our acquisitions more enjoyable. I also went on a patient outing to the cinema. The staff brought the date for the outing forward so that I could go with them prior to my operation.

At Christmas Dr De Maria suggested that I go home for a couple of days so that David and I could spend the time together. I appreciated this and felt more like a person who was in control of my life rather than a patient who needed to be cared for. Though the differences were subtle, the staff were generally more relaxed and friendly and far less judgemental than they had been in Sydney. For instance, though I had a large pressure area and admitted that moving to South Australia had made it worse, no one said that it was my fault. On my previous hospital visits in Sydney, I had always resented the assignment of blame to patients whenever things went awry, such as when my bed broke down.

In the unit at the same time as myself was another ventilator dependent quad called Don. He'd only recently been injured and Don and his mother were still coming to terms with his severe disability. Once I was allowed up, I took the opportunity of speaking to him. I explained how to talk by closing off his glottis and felt pleased when he started practising this. As I was not using my manual wheelchair, I lent it to him. This at least allowed him to go out when he wanted, unlike Paul and I who were unable to leave the hospital grounds for months. I knew how frustrating that was; you seemed to miss out on everything.

In January I was transferred to the spinal unit in the hospital for my operation. I was back in an acute ward with the same blank walls and ceiling with a window behind me. When architects design such units, do they think that because people are sick, they have lost all interest in the world around them? The staff turned my bed partly sideways so that I had a glimpse of sky and trees. The operation went well, and Dr

Nine Expectations and Disappointments

Morris was pleased with the results. I had to lie well over on my side so that I was not lying on the suture line. Though this was not particularly comfortable, it was tolerable because the nurse and orderlies took care to position me correctly. After ten days my drainage tube was removed and I was allowed to have a shower on the trolley lying on my side with the suture covered. What a relief to get my hair washed.

In the bed next to me was Alan, a man who had severe damage to his spinal cord following a recent car accident. No one expected him to recover any use in his arms, but to everyone's surprise he did. I watched as he slowly got some movement back, first in his arms and then his hands. One day he thought he would scratch his forehead, but his coordination was not very good and he hit himself on the forehead instead. The student nurse and I thought this very funny and burst out laughing. Then I asked the nurse to tell Alan a sick joke. It was hard for us to talk directly to each other because of the space between the beds but we would ask the nurses and our visitors to relay messages. We became quite friendly.

There were a number of student nurses working in the ward and though most were considerate, some lacked insight.

'Hello, I didn't know you could talk, so I didn't stop to say hello to you,' the student said. 'Now that was a reasonable assumption, wasn't it?'

I looked at him in disgust. No, I did not think it a reasonable assumption because I *can* talk. What if I could not talk? Am I then to be assigned to the ranks of the non-person to be ignored just because I cannot speak? I could not be bothered replying to such rubbish. He then pointed to my page turner and the book I was reading and said, 'I'm interested in that machine and I want to see it work.'

'I'm still reading this page,' I replied curtly then adding to myself, *I'm not a performing seal.*

Normally I was able to establish a rapport with most people, but there was one group of orderlies who barely acknowledged my presence. They would approach my bed to turn me while having their own conversation, doing their job without even a hello. For the first time since my accident, I felt like a lump of meat, a body in the bed. However, I was hesitant about saying anything because when a nurse asked one of them to be careful with my drainage tube, he seemed to take that as a personal affront. I had the uncomfortable feeling that if I spoke out it might make the situation worse. Therefore, I decided to remain silent as I would only be in the ward for a short time. But after a few days, they did start talking to me, allaying my concerns.

Not long afterwards I returned to the rehabilitation centre. I felt relieved and happy to be back there. Though on the whole I had been well treated in hospital, I had found it a strain being in an acute unit again.

I was devastated to find the following day that the nurse who escorted me had returned to the hospital with my ambubag. The ambubag was my emergency back-up, my security blanket, and I felt very vulnerable without it.

Nine   Expectations and Disappointments

'Why didn't she ask me whether it belonged to the hospital?' I wailed. It was returned promptly the same day.

The ward was now full, but the nurses still tried to attend to my wishes. If had slept badly and wanted to sleep and eat breakfast later, I could. Alan arrived a few days later and I shared a room with Don. I sometimes wondered if he got any rest being in such close proximity to two people on ventilators and the associated noise of alarms and suction machines. The days now stretched out ahead of me, long and empty. I tried to fill in my time by reading and listening to the radio, but some days I could not be bothered doing anything.

I tried to persuade David to visit me every second day knowing how tired he was when previously I been in hospital, but he still visited daily. However, he was desperately lonely even though he had met a few people and Yvonne and Ingrid had invited him to dinner. He tried to fill in his time gardening and paving pathways around the house. Barry and Susanne helped him make more vegetable beds, and he started bringing me fresh salads. This made for a nice change. Though the hospital food was reasonable, I could have a salad or toasted sandwiches if I did not like what was on the menu. The vegetables were always terribly overcooked. There were times though that David looked so miserable that I really did not know what to say to him. At my request, Connie inquired about support groups for carers in our area. We were all surprised and disappointed at discovering that the only group did not accept men.

'That's discrimination,' I said angrily. 'There are a lot of men out there caring for people and they need just as much support as anyone else.'

During this period, I had a lot of time to think. I realised how angry I felt about the pressure area. It should never have occurred in the first place. Had I been able to go home after seven months when I was ready, I believe such a pressure area would not have happened. All my care attendants and nurses at home noted every blemish or red mark on my skin. Had I been allowed to lie from side to side instead of being told that I could not lie on my left side, it would probably have healed before I left hospital the first time. All I got from that episode was a sore shoulder.

I felt that I had missed out on so many things because of the pressure sore and I felt cheated. I had probably made it worse by going to college but had no regrets. After all I'd finished the final year of my course and proved to myself that I could do it. My biggest regret was that I had not returned to work which I would have done at least one day a week had I not had the pressure sore. Having identified my anger, I then let it dissipate like a cloud of smoke.

There were other frustrations too. My pacing program had been disrupted by the move to South Australia and admission to hospital. It seemed that every time I started to build up the hours that I was on the stimulator, something would happen to set me back. For example, after the anaesthetic I had a lot of lung congestion which made it difficult to pace.

Nine Expectations and Disappointments

Though I felt frustrated and disappointed by this lack of progress I decided to wait until I went home to start pacing again properly. David felt frustrated too because he wanted me to progress and accused me of playing around with my pacing program. I was very hurt and angry at his apparent lack of understanding.

I thought about David; he had given up so many things to care for me and though I appreciated this, I also felt guilty. Though I felt no guilt about my accident because what had happened had happened, I wished desperately that it had not impacted on his life too. There were a lot of ifs. If only it had not happened, if I had died, if I were less disabled but the reality was otherwise. Would I have given up work and my life to care for him if our positions were reversed? I did not know. Because I felt guilty, I was over-sensitive to David's criticism of myself or others, and this made it difficult for us to discuss his frustrations. How much longer could I go on feeling responsible for his feelings and decisions as well as my own? I decided not to and felt that huge burden of guilt lift from my shoulders.

'What beautiful hands you've got,' the young nurse exclaimed as she picked them up.

I hastily changed the subject. I did not want to look at my hands lying there lifeless and useless like lumps of dead meat. *They were beautiful once*, I thought. Expressive, graceful hands that could do so much; teach, show others what to do, creative hands that could cook, knit and weave. Hands that could form the graceful shapes of Tai Chi. *What use were they to me now?* I thought bitterly. Of all the losses which I had experienced as a result of my accident, I regretted most the loss of my hands. However, you cannot divorce yourself from a part of your body and I now accept my hands as a part of me. Other people have become my hands and enable me to do the things I want.

The weeks passed slowly and my getting up was delayed for a couple of weeks because a small area on the suture line had not fully healed. I was allowed to start getting up slowly starting with half an hour twice a day and increasing over the next few weeks to two hours. My ordeal was over, and finally I was rid of the pressure sore. I spent these last few weeks talking to other patients and sitting in the garden. Though this was pleasant, the days were increasingly long, and I counted the weeks and days until I could go home.

Of the two years since my accident I had spent eighteen months in hospitals. All I had ever wanted was the opportunity to create a new life with David. Now I could go home and slowly increase the time I was sitting up. As these periods became longer, I would have the opportunity to go out more, meet people and get involved in the local community. At last David and I could have a life together. There would probably be times in the future when I would have to return to hospital but not for a long, long time if I could help it.

I did have one drama during this period. When I was allowed up, I often sat in the garden. Normally there were other patients out there but being close to lunch they'd gone in. Driving across the grass I hit a bump and my chin control

Nine Expectations and Disappointments

bar dropped down knocking the cap off my ventilator tubing. This meant that I was not getting any air to breathe. For a moment I hesitated. Should I let nature take its course? No, I decided that I wanted to live and to have the opportunity to start a new life. I raced to the door which was shut. Fortunately, one of the patient's relatives heard my ventilator alarm and let me in. Then a nurse put her finger over the end of my tracheostomy tube while the other nurses searched the grass for my cap. It was eventually found sitting on my t-shirt. Shortly after this, the occupational therapy department fixed my chin control so that the bar no longer slipped. They also replaced my armrests with ones that gave my arms good support. It was good to finally resolve these problems.

Don went home a few days before me. His mother showed great determination to get him home where he could be with family and friends. He went home six months after his accident. On a bright sunny day two days later, David took me home. I was so happy that I cried. There were so many things that I wanted to do such as finish writing this book. I also looked forward to getting out and meeting new people and doing new things. My new ambition in life was to go dog-sledding. Most things are possible if you are willing to try.

Ten

What's Your Handicap?

Life is too important to be taken seriously.

During my first few weeks at home, I was very tired and slept a lot. I expected to feel tired after a period in hospital. At this stage, I was still only allowed to sit up in the chair for a couple of hours, but I increased this time only very slowly. The nurses and my attendant carers meticulously inspected my suture line every day because none of us wanted it to break down. It was great to be home and to eat fresh vegetables straight from the garden. I felt that I had been given a new lease of life and now all I had to do was organise myself.

One of the first things that I had to organise was another carer. Though Ingrid and Angela continued to come, Lillian being a full-time carer had accepted other clients during the long period that I was in hospital. However, she had kept one day free so that she could work with me. I felt happy about this because I liked Lillian and we had a lot in common. I contacted the coordinator to let her know that I was home and she gave me the names of two attendant carers who would contact me. The first one to do so was Bobbie, a young woman with green eyes. She had done a five-week attendant carers course and appeared confident and responsible. I asked her to start the following Saturday. Again, David had to show her how my machines worked, how to suction me, what to do in the case of an emergency and where things were kept. Whenever I had new carers, David had to go through this procedure and stay around the house until they felt confident about the work.

A short while later, Katherine contacted me and I told her on the phone that I had enough carers at present but that I may need someone to relieve on sick days and holidays. As Lillian was a friend of hers and had told me a little about her, I was interested in a meeting. Katherine arrived, her red hair garnered with turquoise beads. When I asked about her background, she shared her life history with us.

What an interesting woman, I thought, *she is obviously a feminist which isn't a problem, but she seems very intense. I wonder how well she will get on with David?*

We took her phone number and I said that I would contact her if I needed anyone to fill in for the other carers. Shortly after this, Lillian went to join her partner for a few weeks as he was working as a lighthouse keeper on an offshore island. Katherine filled in and in time we both came to like her openness and generosity. Then when Bobbie could no longer come for personal reasons, Katherine took over her hours.

Ten What's Your Handicap?

One of my other priorities was to increase my pacing hours which had been badly disrupted by the move and admission to hospital. I started to do this and also paced during the short period that I was up in the chair. Nothing ever seemed to go smoothly. One day David, Bobbie and I had gone for a short walk around the block to look at the neighbours' gardens. As I was feeling well using the stimulator, we decided not to take the ventilator and left it at home. On the return journey, the transmitter on the stimulator suddenly stopped working. Thinking that it was the battery, David changed it, but there was still no signal. By this stage, Bobbie had started to hand-ventilate me with the ambubag and continued to do so until we reached home where I could be put on the ventilator. David then tried yet another battery but still no signal from the transmitter.

What to do? Dr De Maria was away, so I rang Dr Angelis in Sydney. She concurred with my opinion that the transmitter may need to be sent to America for repair but suggested that I contact the spinal unit in Adelaide first. Then I tried to contact Connie but being the day before Easter she was very busy with patients who were going home and I could not reach her. All weekend I worried about the days that I was not pacing. Would the muscle get lazy? *How long,* I wondered, *would it take to get the transmitter repaired*? When Lillian came, she contacted one of her other clients who was also on a phrenic nerve stimulator and she provided us with the name of the technician who serviced her unit. The following day I contacted Connie who in turn contacted Georgio, the technician, on my behalf. This took quite a lot of phone calls but eventually we tracked him down and David took my transmitter in for Georgio to check. After all that, it turned out to be a flat battery; the transmitter was working fine. What an unlucky coincidence to have three flat batteries in a row.

Though it was a week since I had done any pacing, I was able to do five hours before I started to tire. Over the next two weeks, I rapidly increased my pacing time back to the eight hours that I had been on previously. Then I had another problem. During this period I had continued to slowly increase the time that I was sitting up, but I soon experienced a return of the nausea which I had previously while pacing in my chair. Worse still I started to have dizzy spells and blackouts.

'The settings definitely need checking,' I declared to David. 'I should not be having all this trouble.'

I decided to continue pacing only while I was in bed and not when I was in the chair. David had spoken to Dr Gordon when he'd taken the transmitter into Georgio. Dr Gordon had expressed an interest in assessing me. When Dr De Maria returned to work, I contacted her and discussed this issue. She was very happy to refer me to Dr Gordon who had experience and the technical back up with the phrenic nerve stimulator. In June we went to see Dr Gordon and spent several hours with Georgio while he checked the stimulator settings and changed them to give me a longer breath. Though Dr Angelis had tried to do this in Sydney, she did not have a satisfactory way of measuring the outcome whereas Georgio did.

In addition to altering the stimulator, Georgio also changed my ventilator settings. For a long time, the nurses had noted that I stimulated extra breaths above the rate that the ventilator was set on and this was put down to muscular activity. However, because I had been stimulating extra breaths, I was also hyperventilating. When Georgio altered the ventilator settings I noted that symptoms which I had for some time such as a continuously runny nose, episodes of blurred vision and chronic fatigue almost completely disappeared and only came back if I was ill or physically stressed.

After we finished with Georgio, I met Dr Gordon who showed us the Sleep Unit and said that he would like to assess me again when I started sleeping overnight on the stimulator. They could then measure the amount of oxygen I was receiving and whether I had normal sleep patterns. I agreed to do this. My first goal was to increase my pacing time to ten hours.

While I was in hospital, David had done a lot of work in the garden. A friend had helped him pave the driveway and David had put in pathways which went to the front of our block and part way around the house. He had made garden beds at the front of the house and filled these with old-fashioned roses and small flowering plants. In addition, he'd planted a number of trees. He had also dug out more vegetable beds and was growing a profusion of tomatoes and other vegetables.

Unfortunately, with all this work he had developed tendonitis in his forearm which caused him considerable distress. This meant that he could not do anything heavy and my coming home exacerbated the problem. I persuaded him to see the local doctor who prescribed a course of an anti-inflammatory drugs which helped a little, but it was several months before the soreness in his arms disappeared.

In April my mother came down from Queensland for a short visit. It was good to see her looking so well and to hear that she was still actively involved with environmental issues in her area. My mother was a keen bird watcher and would get up early every morning to go for a walk and watch birds. I didn't not share her passion though I did recognise several different types of birds. For a joke I told her that I could only recognise magpies, of which there were plenty around Strathalbyn. The weather was mild and sunny, and we often sat out in the garden. Because I was restricted to four hours per day of sitting in my chair, we could not go far, but David took her on drives on the mornings that I had my shower. It seemed that every time my mother visited me, I was spending long hours in bed.

On my birthday, however, we took a picnic and went to the local park. There we spent a pleasant afternoon under the shade of the gum trees watching the ducks swimming in the river. During her stay, my mother learnt to suction me, and this gave David more freedom to be in the garden or to go up the street without worrying that I was all right.

It had become increasingly obvious that we needed some sort of alarm system which would allow either David or my carers to be contacted if I had a problem with the stimulator which has no alarm. Particularly if they were outside. But just what sort of alarm was the problem? When I had started the pacing program in Sydney one of the medical technicians had suggested putting an alarm button on the chin control of my electric wheelchair. However, I had rejected this idea because the chin control tended to slip down and I worried that putting something else there would make the problem worse. Also, I would only be able to use the alarm when I was in that particular chair. Nor could I use the alarm if the chin control was swung up out of the way; if I was using the computer, for example. We discussed this problem again with the occupational therapists at the rehabilitation centre, but it seemed the only things which might be suitable were voice operated alarms. This meant that if David was working out in the garden, he would be listening to every conversation I had and every radio program I might be listening to. Hardly satisfactory.

One day David went to a nursery to buy some garden plants. When he entered the nursery, no one was in attendance, but a nurseryman arrived shortly even though David had not heard any alarms nor pushed any bells. When other customers arrived, David noted that the nurseryman was wearing a beeper that went off as new people entered the premises. David asked about this and it appeared that when a customer walked in, they passed through an infrared beam setting off beepers carried by the staff. He then gave David the name and phone number of the man who had installed the system.

At this David made contact and explained our problem. Several ideas were accumulated and a system design was put forward. One was where I could activate by pushing a button on a small unit with my head. This unit sent a signal to a transmitter which in turn set off a beeper carried by David. My unit could be pinned to my pillow or attached with Velcro to either of the headrests on my wheelchairs. This worked extremely well.

Whenever I came home, David and I went through a period of readjustment. Both of us were tired and he was frustrated by being unable to do much work around the house or in the garden because of his tendonitis. But having been in hospital, I'd accumulated care hours, so I increased the periods that my attendant carers were coming in order to give David some relief. To my surprise, some of the nurses questioned this decision. They thought that there might be too many people coming and that David and I did not have enough time to ourselves. I found this irritating. Firstly, it was my life to organise in whichever way possible and secondly because my carers enabled me to do things that I could not do otherwise. Also, my normal care hours were limited because they were paid for by a government funded scheme. This meant that David was with me for far longer than most couples spent together.

There were times when my carers and the nurses continued to annoy me by pinning my ventilator tubing to my pillow in such a manner that it dragged on my neck. This was despite being asked to do otherwise. It also caused me a great deal of concern that they had trouble plugging the wheelchair battery into the back of the ventilator. All it needed was a little care and time to look and see which way round the plug went; easy enough when done properly. As these plugs cost over one hundred dollars each, I worried that the plug might get broken. This had happened in Sydney through one of my carers trying to force the plug in the wrong way. Replacement of such items was an added expense that I could do without.

There were times too when the people caring for me inadvertently caused irritation to David. Such as not putting things back where they found them or omitting to replace the things that were used, like toilet paper in the bathroom. There was a fine line between caring and doing things for me without causing disruption and excessive irritation to the person that I shared my life with, namely David.

It was increasingly obvious despite the extra help that David needed a break and as I had enough care hours, I persuaded him to take a holiday. At first, he was reluctant to go because he felt so responsible for my welfare but in the end, he decided to go to Sydney for ten days. In order to organise everything, we had a lunch for my care attendants, and they all brought a plate which saved a lot of work for David. It also gave them an opportunity to meet each other - some for the first time. We organised a roster for the period when David would be away and spent the rest of the afternoon talking. It was such a good day we decided to have such lunches again in the future. A couple of weeks later David went to Sydney and spent time visiting friends and going out to lunch with old work colleagues. On returning he admitted it had been very hard giving up work. Though he missed the stimulation and companionship of Sydney, this holiday had been the right thing to do.

How I wish that I could have gone with him, to share a holiday in the way that we used to. Still I was at home and despite a bit of irritation, felt I could trust the people who were looking after me. Barry and Susanne stayed with me on the first weekend. Susanne had learnt how to suction me and had also helped to dress and undress me. Initially this felt strange, but as she was like a member of our family, I soon became comfortable with her helping me in this way.

Barry was quite happy to feed me and usually offered to do so whenever we had meals together. After that, different carers came according to the roster and apart from developing a urinary tract infection, everything went smoothly. They also made me special meals; Ingrid bought a crayfish, Angela made a quiche and I discovered that Katherine could whip-up an excellent curry.

The weather was wet much of the time David was away, so I did not mind staying at home. I felt very unwell with the urinary tract infection and had to take a course of antibiotics. A few weeks later I felt unwell yet again; this time it was more serious. I would wake in the night feeling burning hot and thirsty and I fainted whenever out of bed. The local doctor contacted Dr De Maria about these recurrent urinary infections. The district nurse, Wendy, was also worried and suggested that we talk with the nurse continence adviser. These were nurses who specialised in bladder and bowel care and the problems associated with incontinence. I felt that this was a good idea and after discussing the details with Wendy and me, the adviser made several suggestions. This led to a different system of bladder care which seemed to work reasonably well, though I did develop another urinary tract infection a few months later following a bout of gastric upset.

When I was in the rehabilitation centre, the occupational therapists had made some alterations to my wheelchairs and had also agreed to alter my commode chair. So when I went back for a check-up, David took my commode chair down to the Occupational Therapy department. On the way, he met one of the OTs who admired a Fair Isle jumper that he was wearing.

'That is a beautiful jumper that you've got on.'

'Yes,' David said proudly. 'Hilary knitted it for me. She knits with her teeth, you know?' The somewhat impossible idea of teeth knitting had been a long-standing joke.

David was dumbfounded when the OT replied, 'Does she really? How marvellous.'

This story was too amusing not to relay to others. Katherine, who was also a photographer, took it one step further by borrowing her partner's knitting and took several photos of me with the knitting in my mouth. The nurses asked for a copy which they put up on their notice board under the heading, *Knitting Champion at Work*.

During my stay in hospital, I had shared with Connie what

it was like to become disabled, what helped and what did not. We talked about grieving and living with the reality of a disability. I was in a position where I had worked with people with disabilities in a professional capacity, both as a nurse and counsellor, only to become disabled myself. In addition, I was willing to share my thoughts and feelings with other professionals because I believed that with a greater understanding of all the aspects, they would be better able to help people in that condition. I believed that I had the skills and knowledge which enabled me to do that.

Later Connie contacted me at home to ask if I was willing to talk to the other social workers at the rehabilitation centre. I also agreed to speak the same evening to a group run by Connie for friends and relatives of people with a spinal cord injury. David and I went to the rehabilitation centre and talked at length with the social workers about my disability and how it had affected both of us. Though not everyone there was working with spinal cord injury clients.

As we had some spare time before our evening presentation, we were able to talk with Alan and catch up with the news of other patients. Don was doing well at home and started to get good head control. He'd been back to hospital once but was currently fine. I was pleased for him and hoped that he continued to progress at home.

In the evening David and I talked to the friends and relatives' group about living with the reality of being disabled from a personal viewpoint. Patients had also been invited and Alan was there. I shared some of my experiences with the group and told the story of how Amy and Rolland pushed me around the golf course in the Sydney hospital with Amy hand-ventilating me and Rolland pushing.

'What I want to know,' Alan piped up, 'with all those people pushing you around, what's your handicap?'

Some weeks later I gave a talk about The Ventilated Client for the care attendants training course and was asked to talk to the next group. It would have been good to do more, but people often saw me as a person with needs rather than someone with skills to share. At times I found this very irritating but decided to persist; to keep offering my skills to others.

David and I also became more involved in the local community and started going to meetings such as Trees for Life. This was a fairly large group who promoted the growing and planting of native trees in the local area. It was a friendly group and I felt comfortable being with them. Yvonne and her husband invited David to Rotary meetings and we went to one of their dinners. Unfortunately, we had to rush home at the end because the battery for my ventilator went flat. From then on, we went to other functions, getting to know people and being involved in community activities.

As my sitting up time increased, we also started going out for drives in the country, visited friends and went out to dinner. We also invited people to dinner with us and gradually our circle of friends and acquaintances increased. Being a rural community, people with similar interests tended to know each other; farming people, craftspeople etc. When David, Katherine and I visited Hahndorf one day, I was amused but not surprised that Lillian heard of our visit to Althope Island where she was lighthouse keeping with her partner.

Shortly after he returned from Sydney, David hurt his back working in the garden. With me to care for it was very difficult for him to rest. I did what I could and as I still had extra care hours, I asked a friend of Bobbie's to help put me back to bed in the afternoon. However, I was concerned when David complained of increasing numbness in his leg and persuaded him to see the local doctor. The doctor diagnosed a prolapsed disc in his lower back and told David to go home and rest, then laughed. Though he was sympathetic, he knew that in our circumstances such rest was impossible for David.

This back problem prevented David from doing other things such as gardening and of course laying paving was out of the question. The pain and numbness continued to come and go for some months. He became quite despondent, especially when he looked at all the work he had to do. I wished that I could have cared for him rather than the other way around. It was a trying time for both of us, and though I tried to be supportive and less demanding we tended to fight; often over trivial things. We both needed an outlet.

David expressed to Katherine an interest in learning to play a musical instrument, so she lent him her flute and some music. Though he had never played a musical instrument before, David was soon playing simple tunes. He found this so enjoyable and relaxing that he bought his own flute and continued to practice most days. I started writing poetry as a way of expressing some thoughts that were still too painful to share with others.

As David's back improved, he started doing more work. Bobbie suggested that her husband, Damien, who was out of work, come and help him. He came one day and started helping David connect some stormwater pipes to our recently installed rain tanks. Just under one of the downpipes near the concrete slab at the back of the carport was a rough piece of concrete which David and Damien decided to dig up. Damien could not find the crowbar which he was looking for and picked up a wooden handled mattock instead. I watched as he swung the mattock over his head and smashed through the concrete. The next minute, Damien was covered in a cloud of sparks and smoke. I was surprised to see him still standing. We looked at each other.

'Shit!' we both exclaimed.

Damien had cut through the main electricity supply to our house. There had been nothing to indicate that there were electricity cables only a few centimetres under the concrete. I was relieved that Damien had not been killed. Bobbie and David came running to see what had happened. Then we had to get the damage repaired. Fortunately, David had purchased a small generator some months earlier as an emergency power back up because the repairs took the best part of a day.

We continued to have ups and downs, and David went through periods of self-doubt. Was he caring for me adequately? Was I better looked after by other people? This was not helped by people making insensitive remarks which inferred that he had an easy life. I tended to ignore such remarks because I found them ridiculously inappropriate, but David was deeply hurt by them. Being a full-time carer is never easy. He has the constant worry about my welfare.

We both knew that I could die if something went wrong with either the ventilator or stimulator. His sleep was often broken because I may have needed suctioning several times during the night. Though I tried not to do it too often, there were times when he was about to relax only to find he needed to attend to me. My care attendants were only with me for a very limited number of hours.

When David did go out, he had to be very conscious of the time so that he got back before my attendants finished their shift. This also restricted where he went and what he did. In addition, he had to do all the things that we used to share such as shopping, cooking and gardening. The worth of full-time carers is rarely recognised until they burn out, give up or get sick. I worried that this might happen to him. Though I tried to give him support, there were times when I found this difficult. If it were not for the situation we found ourselves in, and my disability, then he would not have all this stress. I was relieved when a carers' group had its first meeting in Strathalbyn because it gave David the opportunity to share his difficulties with other carers. People worried about my needs, but David needed as much support as I did.

Ten   What's Your Handicap?

In July I was sad to hear the news of Harry's death. He died from a heart attack. I thought of his mother and how hard she had fought to get everything organised to take him home. She had supported and encouraged Harry in every way possible and I believed that she could not have done more. Harry had gone home for several months and celebrated his twenty-first birthday at home surrounded by his family and friends. I hoped that though it was such a short time, his mother felt that it was all worthwhile. Living the rest of your life as a high dependency quadriplegic is never easy.

In July, Lea came to stay for a brief visit. It was so good to see her; she will always be someone very special to me. We took her out for a drive and lunch in a very pleasant old pub. I continued to miss my friends in Sydney though we kept in touch by letter and phone. David's back was improving and he started doing more things outside. The garden was full of soursobs, a pretty plant with a yellow flower but a real pest to get rid of. We had far too many to weed by hand, so David sprayed them. We bought more roses and fruit trees and planted them. Then we had a pergola built along the north side of the house. We were to grow grapevines on it which would give us shade in the summer and sun in the winter. I kept busy writing this book, catching up with correspondence and preparing notes for various talks. When the weather was nice, I would go into the garden whilst David worked.

At the end of July, I reached my ten hours of pacing on the stimulator and started pacing overnight. The first week was hard for both of us as I tended to wake frequently needing suctioning. Then neither of us could get back to sleep. We both became very tired and ratty with each other. I also found that it was more tiring pacing during the night and had to reduce my pacing hours. However, the second week was better; I usually woke only once or twice for suctioning and increased my pacing time again. My aim is to be on the stimulator twenty-four hours a day by the middle of next year. Hopefully I'll start sleeping through the night again because David is suffering from broken sleep and some days he is extremely tired.

We will have to arrange for some respite care at the local hospital in the near future as David needs another break. Despite being a small local hospital, the sort of hospital where one goes to be born or to die, they have agreed to take me. This is in marked contrast to the regional hospital where Don lived which refused to treat him for anything because he was a high-level quadriplegic on a ventilator. It seems ridiculous that some health professionals feel that they cannot cope with people like Don and myself. Yet we can live at home with people like David and Don's mother who have no formal training whatsoever. I will be pleased to go into the local hospital if only to prove that such institutions do not need specialised units to care for people like me.

In August it was David's birthday, but he was not looking forward to the event when he thought of all the things he'd not achieved. David also felt down when he thought of all the past birthdays which we had celebrated together and regretted

Ten What's Your Handicap?

I could no longer do the same things for him. I tried hard to make the day enjoyable. Lillian bought a chocolate cake and we decorated it with sparklers. Then we cooked a special lunch for him. But he was still very depressed. A few days later on a wet and windy day, we drove up to the Barossa Valley for a leisurely lunch at a good restaurant. We both enjoyed the outing and the excellent food in spite of the weather. Life is still worth living.

I know David still keenly felt the loss of his career, but as a person he has so many good qualities to be proud of. There were so many things that we had planned to do together, especially travel, which now we could not afford. If we had the money, then travel would be possible for both of us. Perhaps one day I will be able to go dog sledding and visit my sister in England. For me travel means a lot of extra expense such as a nurse escort if I fly, the staying in hotel accommodation and the hire of equipment.

Though I still cling to the hope that we may travel together again one day, I no longer have the desire to live to an advanced age. I had always thought that David and I would grow old together and enjoy an active old age. But now I do not want to live that long. There will come a time when David will find the constant burden of caring for me too great. Even though he has promised to be there for as long as I need him, I will not keep him to that promise. Also, I would like him to have a time in his life when he is free from care, free to travel again. If he travels with the memory of me, then we will be together.

Eleven

Looking forward

*"Yesterday is but today's memory,
tomorrow is but today's dream."*
Khalil Gibran

It is now two and a half years since that fateful day in February 1989 when I fell off my bike, and I feel that I have made a long and difficult journey since then. During that time, I have changed from at first wishing that I had died because dying would have been so easy. I did not want to come back into the real world. Coming back meant, for me, facing the reality of my paralysis and my inability to breathe. Dying was preferable to being kept alive on a machine.

Then for a long time afterwards, I felt very ambivalent about my survival and often unconcerned, for example, when my tubing fell apart and I could not breathe. After all, I was living on borrowed time. It was not until I had the phrenic nerve stimulator implanted that I felt that I had any choice as to whether I lived or died. In agreeing to the operation, I decided that I did in fact want to live and to have the opportunity of creating a new life with David.

No one can say how long I may live. I could die tomorrow or live a normal life span, and in this regard I'm no different to anyone else. Anyone of us could die suddenly from a heart attack or an accident, for example. I do not worry unduly about my survival because I am not afraid of dying. Others do worry and feel responsible for my welfare. I wish it was otherwise.

Sometimes the question arises as to whether people such as me who are in need of a high level of care and attention should be living at home. My experience has shown that this is not only possible but also have a much better quality of life. I believe that it is quality not quantity of life that is important. I found the first year that I spent in hospital following my accident extremely trying. It was even more psychologically traumatising for me because I spent the whole time in the acute care section of the ward. I was usually with people who were recently injured and their grieving relatives. But as I progressed, I had less and less in common with them. I wished that I could have been in the rehabilitation section of the ward and have talked with the other patients. I have heard of other ventilated people in other hospitals being similarly treated. It seems to me as a high-level quadriplegic that having saved our lives, medical and nursing staff are unsure as to what to do with us. We spend long periods languishing, unnecessarily, in hospital, before we go home. Eventually when we do go home, the services we need are not always available. Very often we end up being looked after by people who are untrained.

Despite the fact that neither David nor my care attendants received much instruction regarding my care before I went home, I feel safer being cared for by them and the district nurses than I did when in hospital. This is because I have good carers who are familiar with my needs and who take the time to listen. Being able to choose my own care attendants and have a stable relationship with them is very important. I have met most of the district nurses, and they are also familiar with my routine and needs. Having people who are familiar with my care relieves some of the burden on David who has always had to educate new people. It was unfortunate he never received such education himself. It is also unfortunate that we never had the opportunity to go out for day trips or to go home for the weekend prior to my first discharge from the hospital.

Had there been better organisation and some proper discharge planning by the hospital in Sydney, I believe that I could have left hospital when I was ready, seven to eight months after my accident. Instead, I spent many more months in hospital becoming increasingly bored and depressed and developing pressure sores. Perhaps I might have developed pressure areas at home, but I doubt this because everyone who has and does care for me at home checks my skin meticulously.

There were a number of factors as to why the pressure area on by thigh took so long to heal and eventually need surgery.

No doubt some people will say that I should not have gone to college. I have no regrets about returning to college because not only did it help restore my self-esteem which was shattered by the accident, but it proved that I could still do things that I wanted to do. I did finish my course and I now have a Graduate Diploma in Administration from a major university.

The consequence of my accident has involved considerable costs, not only to myself but also to David. There has been the personal cost of changing from being a very busy and active person to someone who is severely disabled and reliant on others. We have both had to make major changes to our lives such as giving up jobs and careers, changing house and living on reduced financial circumstances.

There are so many things that we used to do together which are no longer possible such as skiing, cycling, and bushwalking. Even to go out for the day means thinking about whether the access is good and taking suction equipment and the airbag with us among other things. I think that it is this constant worry about my well-being together with the lack of sleep and time for relaxation that is most wearing for David. I worry about him getting sick or having an accident partly because I cannot care for him and partly because I could no longer live at home if he did.

Though I do receive some attendant care hours through a federally funded scheme, they are inadequate for our needs and neither of us has the freedom to do the things we would like. Even if I received twenty-four-hour care this would still be less than the cost of me being in an institution. David saves the government a considerable amount of money through his willingness to give up his job to look after me. For this, he receives three dollars a day. Because I receive a superannuation pension he is not eligible for the full carer's pension, nor are we eligible for any fringe benefits. David's skills and professional expertise are lost to society. I wonder how many others are in similar situations.

There are considerable strains on our relationship and we continue to go through periods of ups and downs. Our marriage has survived so far because it was very strong prior to my accident and I believe that it will continue for many years yet. However, I dread the day when David feels he can no longer care for me because being able to live at home and be with him is so important to me. I no longer have any desire to live into advanced old age because it will become increasingly difficult for him. There were so many things that we planned to do together and it has been very hard to give up those dreams. But I hope he will survive me and have enough healthy and active years in which to do the things he wants.

Becoming disabled always involves a lot of pain and grieving for the many, many losses in your life. I felt that having survived my accident I had two choices; either to perpetually grieve and regret what had happened or to learn to live with my disability. I chose the latter not because I was particularly brave but because it was the only reasonable choice that I could make. Fortunately, I was a very self-aware person who had learnt to accept and like myself, warts and all, prior to my accident. In addition, I had rich and varied life experiences as well as many skills and knowledge of grief and disability.

I was able to use all this firstly to accept myself as someone who was physically unable to help herself and later to accept myself as a person with a physical disability. The most difficult things which I had to come to terms with were my loss of independence, the loss of the use of my hands and the guilt which I felt about the impact of my accident on David's life. I have never spent a lot of time regretting what happened or wishing things were otherwise because I would rather use the energy that I have to do other things. Life is too important to waste.

Right from the beginning, David made an unselfish commitment to care for me and to be there for as long as I need him. Would I have done the same for him? I do not know. David is of course, not just my principle carer, he is also my husband, my lover and my best friend. Despite his own personal losses and grief, he has continued to support and care for me in a way that has helped me to regain my self-esteem and to value myself once again as a person.

I have also been fortunate too, in having some very good friends who continued to visit me the whole time that I was in hospital. This was no mean feat in itself, as many had to travel a long way to do so. Though I have only mentioned a few names in this book, there were many others including David's friends and colleagues who gave and continue to give us considerable support and understanding. Though we have moved away from Sydney, we keep in touch with most of them either by letter or phone.

Since my accident, I have renewed old friendships and made new ones, perhaps because I still care about others. I was therefore rather surprised when a colleague who had been overseas visited me about eleven months after my accident and stated that I must have lost a lot of friends as a result of my accident. No one whom I would call a friend has deserted me. Likewise, all the members of the team with which I was working were very supportive and also raised money on my behalf. I still regret I did not have the opportunity to go back and work with them.

Work has always been very important to me and even at home I used to relax by doing something: knitting, craft, cooking, gardening or reading. One of the hardest things I found in hospital was how to fill in my time. Being able to use a computer was a great help and still is. Now that I live at home I find many more things to do, but there are still empty hours in the day. David and I envy each other because he wishes that he has more time to do things and I wish that I could do something physically active.

We are slowly rebuilding our lives in our new home. In some ways, this might have been easier to do had we remained in Sydney where we had friends and contacts. It is possible for instance, that we may have both been able to do some part-time or voluntary work. However, we would have faced greater financial hardship. We believe that we made the right decision in moving to a small country town. We enjoy a reasonable quality of life here.

Moving to a country town has also meant owning our own home, being able to grow vegetables and live more within our means. Barry and Susanne are regular visitors, and we are making new friends with people who live in Strathalbyn. As we become more involved with the local community and with other groups, I feel confident that I will find more worthwhile things to do. I believe that I still have a lot to give and to share. Being disabled does not mean that you can no longer do things. Instead, you may have to find different ways of doing them.

No doubt some people will ask whether it has all been worth it. Certainly, the costs have been very high. Not only the considerable personal costs to both myself and to David but also the costs to society.

There are the costs of the loss of our skills and knowledge to the workforce as well as loss of revenue from two tax-paying members of the community. There are the enormous health costs of keeping a person such as myself alive and in hospital for extended periods of time. There are also the ongoing costs of providing me with equipment and aids as well as care which enable me not only to live but also to have a reasonable quality of life. We live in a society where life is considered to be precious and worth saving, but we are often appalled at the ongoing cost of the care for the person whose life we have saved. Dying for me was a very pleasant experience and I think that I shall always wonder what would have happened if I had not been resuscitated.

I find it hard to answer the question whether I should have lived or died because it raises so many difficult moral and legal issues. I leave it for the reader of this book to think about those issues. Despite my severe physical disability, I am recreating my life. Most of the time life is enjoyable and satisfying.

All I want to say is that if by surviving my accident I have been able to touch upon and enhance the lives of others then my living has been worthwhile.

In early 1993 Hilary was diagnosed with breast cancer. She died of that disorder the following year.

IN MEMORIAM

Tomorrow trees will dapple with shade
and violet's scent quiet country lanes.
Celandines will glisten with pure gold
and jam-jars with frog's spawn be filled.
Children will paint their Easter eggs
and April will shower with rain.
And I shall remember you once again
the dark-haired child of every spring.

Gill Moore (sister)

www.ingramcontent.com/pod-product-compliance
Lightning Source LLC
Chambersburg PA
CBHW021100080526
44587CB00010B/324